Graduate

The Reality of What to Expect on the Other Side of a Business Degree

Grosvenor House
Publishing Limited

All rights reserved
Copyright © Soukayna Ikhiche, 2024

The right of Soukayna Ikhiche to be identified as the author of this
work has been asserted in accordance with Section 78
of the Copyright, Designs and Patents Act 1988

The book cover is copyright to Soukayna Ikhiche

This book is published by
Grosvenor House Publishing Ltd
Link House
140 The Broadway, Tolworth, Surrey, KT6 7HT.
www.grosvenorhousepublishing.co.uk

This book is sold subject to the conditions that it shall not, by way of
trade or otherwise, be lent, resold, hired out or otherwise circulated
without the author's or publisher's prior consent in any form of
binding or cover other than that in which it is published and
without a similar condition including this condition being
imposed on the subsequent purchaser.

A CIP record for this book
is available from the British Library

ISBN 978-1-80381-798-9

Leadership is lifting a person's vision to high sights, the raising of a person's performance to a higher standard, the building of a personality beyond its normal limitations.

—Peter Drucker

Author

Soukayna Ikhiche is a 25-year-old Moroccan/Italian Sales Professional who has lived in Morocco, Italy, France, UK, Ireland, and Germany.

During her studies, Soukayna has been working closely with several companies, consulting them on their business expansion strategy, and travelling abroad for international events.

After completing her Master of Science in International Business Engineering in Montpellier and obtaining a second degree in Business & Entrepreneurship, Soukayna relocated to Berlin. There she started her career in B2B Tech Sales in the start-up environment, before successfully joining Google as an Account Manager.

At Google, she discovered a passion for digital marketing and personal branding, which led her to building her own personal brand on LinkedIn.

Fluent in several languages, with an extremely international background, Soukayna has successfully built her own way into B2B Sales by displaying exceptional business and marketing acumen, powerful soft skills, and a unique ambition to grow into the best version of herself.

Contents

Acknowledgements		ix
Introduction		xi
Chapter 1	What Really Happens After College	1
Chapter 2	Your First Business Job Glossary	12
Chapter 3	Applying for Your First Job	24
Chapter 4	Acing Any Job Interview	35
Chapter 5	Getting Your First Job	52
Chapter 6	Dealing With Uncertainty	64
Chapter 7	The Power of Self-Accountability	75
Chapter 8	The Power of Mindset	86
Chapter 9	Focusing on What Matters	110
Chapter 10	Navigating Today's Job Market	120
Conclusion		135

Acknowledgements

You're probably wondering how it all started, and what is the story behind this book.

It sounds slightly surreal to think of someone somewhere in the world reading these lines, so let me take you with me on a journey to explain how it all started.

I started writing *Graduate* on a cloudy Saturday in Berlin, sitting at my favorite Einstein Kaffee, with a hot chai latte in hand.

On my return from a trip to London, I began thinking about how many students currently step out from a Business degree and walk into the job market with no clue about how to apply for a job, network, or build their careers.

In most cases, they simply faced the consequences of what college might have not taught them.

And it made me think about how much I wish I had read somewhere what I could expect from my first years after college.

So *Graduate* began as a few questions on a notebook page, which then became chapters.

And before I knew it, I was writing my first book.

Introduction

September 2016.

I will never forget my first year of college; the memory is still freshly vivid in my mind.

I was 18 years old when I moved by myself to Montpellier, and I remember that first day as if it was yesterday: packing the car with my parents, driving all the way through the city with my dad, getting my first keys in the college dormitory.

These are the kind of memories that stay with you forever.

Not many of us had a clear idea of what we were walking into when applying for that degree, joining that university, or choosing those courses.

Then we found ourselves sitting in the classroom on the first day of university, with the conviction that this was the beginning of the rest of our adulthood life.

The biggest misconception of the education system in our century is unrealistically expecting a 17-18-year-old to choose a degree, by making them believe that such a choice will dictate the rest of their life.

It's a misconception that only adds pressure to the level of stress and fear of failure which many young students are probably struggling with already.

If you are going through this at the moment, or are about to step up into college or university, this book is a letter from the future from someone who has already walked that same road and who figured out a few things early enough to make it all work well.

Chapter 1

What Really Happens After College

But wait, what does actually happen after college?

This was one of the most frequent questions I would ask myself when I was in college, and it's a great one to ask, I admit.

If you are currently a student, the answer to this question for you is what will play a big outcome in the beginning of your professional career.

Now that I am on the other side of the spectrum, there are certainly a couple of things that I wish I had known before dreaming of a smooth transition into the real business world.

What tends to happen is that the typical saying *'Get a degree so you can find a good job'* gets lost in translation, because nobody seems to speak about how to really find a job.

Or how to keep it. And how to assess if it's the right job for you.

And also *when* is it actually going to feel right.

Ah, and *what* to do when it actually doesn't anymore.

Interesting, right?

So, the question here is: to what extent does a Business degree really prepare you for what's next?

And I am going to be honest with you on this one.

It does help in theory, and you will learn a couple of things on accounting, management, and economics that will help some other things make more sense.

However, what I will share with you in the next pages is exactly what school does not teach, and why you should learn these concepts yourself if you want to master the power of standing out.

I used to believe that there would be a very smooth transition between studying and working.

I mean, I had everything in place for it to happen, right?

I graduated with good grades, and I already had the possibility to put my skills into practice — what could go wrong?

The answer is pretty much everything can go wrong. Or if you want to be as pessimistic as Murphy would be: if one thing can go wrong, then it certainly will.

What happens after college is simply summed up in one word — *life*.

If you have attended university, at some point you will have stumbled on a couple of classes teaching you about how to write a CV, a cover letter, or how to prepare for your first interview rounds.

However, you'd be luckier than most of us if you addressed topics such soft skills, the psychology of interviewing, impostor syndrome, salary negotiation, career path progression, and the importance of setting realistic goals for yourself.

In other words, how to figure out *what* you want from your professional life.

If you're like the majority of us who are new to such terms, do not worry. I have to admit that I learned those by myself too, in my own timing.

The reality of completing your Business degree is that you'll very likely transition into a full-time job in a company that you will hopefully like enough to decide to stick with for a while.

Interesting shift of perspective, right?

"Wait, what? I should like the company? What do you mean, that I can leave just for not liking how things feel in my work environment?"

Yes, and *especially* for that reason —but let's get there at the right time.

Once you have graduated, and if you have had the chance to do a couple internships (which I have to admit, do help to make the transition smoother), you will be making your way into a full-time job, and often hoping to land the job of your dreams at the first attempt.

But in reality, you do not know what the job of your dreams is, nor if it will match your expectations.

You probably haven't even thought of what your own expectations are at this point, or spoken to people who are on the other side of the spectrum.

I went from working as a student to joining the start-up environment, selling software to B2B, and then switching into large sales within Google. And along the way I have found out what *really* helps you make your way in the professional world.

Connect with people who are doing that job already

One of the best things to do after completing university is to leverage your network, or your network's network, to connect with people who might be already working at that specific company, or performing the job you might want to apply for.

This is one of the best ways to gain an insider's point of view on the job, the daily tasks, and the responsibilities of that person in their day-to-day life.

I have often used *LinkedIn* to do so, by adding into my network the people who were already where I wanted to be as a next step, and then sending them a message to start a conversation with them.

This will not only give you answers, but also introduce you to the art of *networking*, which we will get into later.

These people will be your mentors and will often serve as a strategic point in your development, besides allowing you to save yourself the hassle of making a couple of mistakes on the way.

They can share valuable learnings from their own experience with you.

Treasure the advice they give you, and do not be afraid to ask them to have a virtual coffee and speak more in detail about the best traits to have or develop in order to succeed at that specific job.

When you are no longer a student any more, you will very quickly be confronted with a shift from theory to practice, and leveraging your network is the best way to smooth the transition and facilitate your understanding of what is expected of you at work.

You can also leverage such connections to prepare for job interviews, especially if you can reach out to people who are already working in the company you are aiming for.

Most of the time – and if they are willing enough to do it – this can also earn you a referral, or they may push your application by mentioning your name to a decision-maker within the recruitment team, which might speed things up for you.

However, my tip here from a sales professional is: never make it sound as if you are only reaching out because you need them to do something for you.

Honestly, you should not reach out to anyone like that in the first place.

Reach out to people and humbly ask them to educate you by sharing their experience, be kind and compassionate, and most of all absorb all of the information which they share, so that you can leverage it for your own development.

I advise you to ask them about their own vision of growth in that specific role, or in other words, how did/do they see themselves evolving within the company after a couple of years.

This will give you a very fair and honest understanding of what can be possible as a next milestone, and might also inspire you to think a bit further down the line about which road you might want to explore in your career.

The ability to connect with people, listen to them, and gain insights from their experience, is one of the biggest treasures you will ever have. And if you can get it for free, you've stumbled into a goldmine.

Set your own expectations

The biggest investment you can make to gain clarity at any step in your career, is to sit down with pen and paper and write down the things that are *important* to you.

Structure is one of the best ways to avoid walking into the unknown with too many questions in your mind, and setting down your expectations will help you understand exactly what it is that you are seeking.

When we are starting any new chapter of our life, or jumping into something we have not experienced before, we do not know what will happen.

Yet one thing we can surely do is prepare ourselves in the best way possible.

The transition between university and your first job is something that can be prepared for.

If you write down the things you want, you will have a clearer idea of the direction in which you aim to head, and the people you can go to for questions and advice.

The biggest life-changing tip in my career has been developing the curiosity to ask, and the ability to ignore the feeling of fear that came with forcing myself out of my comfort zone.

And the only way I could do that was by writing down my interests, expectations, things that motivated me, and where I could see myself in the next 6, 12, 24 months.

The next step was finding people who had already walked that road, and reaching out to ask for their experience and advice.

I started showing up at events and conferences where those people were, so that I could connect and learn from them, putting myself out there and networking my way to success.

And that changed everything.

Be proactive in taking the lead

Most of the time we tend to think that we lack the experience to take the lead on something, so we don't do it.

It's hard to overcome this fear and convince ourselves that our experience, no matter how small it looks to us, is actually valuable.

Acknowledging that is the first step to successfully taking the lead.

If you devise to invest in your personal growth, you will often find yourself confronted with the choice of taking new initiatives and stepping into unknown situations.

Being proactive or leading doesn't mean you must have all the answers beforehand, but only that you're strong enough to be comfortable with not knowing.

Transitioning from your education to the professional world means exactly that.

The more you train yourself to come up with new ideas and take a step forward to making an impact, the quicker you will get used to stepping out of your comfort zone.

Being a proactive student can be anything you make out of it — stepping up to represent the class, leading a new initiative to solve an issue, finding companies that are eager to enrol in an internship exchange programme, leading a presentation on how developing your social brand can help you boost your career. Anything.

One rule of thumb I lived by as a student was to always bring a touch of what I used to do outside of class — into the class.

All of us have skills and passions that can simplify each other's lives or elevate each other, so don't hesitate to put those skills on the table and proactively offer to make them part of everyone's learning.

In the worst case scenario, you'll have to take no for an answer.

In the best one, you'll skyrocket your leadership skills.

Network as if your life depended on it

You'll surely stumble upon the word networking an infinite number of times in the next chapters.

The biggest and most rewarding investment of time and resources you will make will be being in the right places, with the right people, at the right time.

I used to think networking was something only those whose parents had a network could get access to. I couldn't have been more wrong.

Your network is a reflection of how proactive you have been in seeking the right connections.

You are defined by the people you spend most of your time with, so why not make sure you're around the most inspiring, empowering, and successful people you could be around?

Networking as a student will put you far ahead of someone who has never done this before.

It's mind-blowing to think that many people pay an incredible amount of money to access private business schools in order to leverage a network of people that they could certainly build for themselves, if they simply invested time in doing so.

The advantage of building your own network is the outstanding amount of self-growth that comes with it.

The ability to search for events that can bring you knowledge and growth, create the right circumstances to take you there, and present yourself as your most confident version, are all invaluable life skills.

I used to work on the weekends in order to make extra money to fly abroad to attend events that resonated with my interests and ambitions, which most of the time were free.

There is often this idea that you need a lot of resources or the right connections to be part of this environment. You don't.

It all starts with you.

I spent a lot of time on platforms such as Eventbrite, searching for professional events around me or abroad, so that I could attend them and learn from the people who were there.

And even when the event didn't end up being what I expected, I had built something incredibly valuable in the process: my self-confidence, my connections, and the ability to learn about what was happening out there in the real world — outside of the classroom.

You'll never be this young again

We often think that being young and inexperienced is something negative in your career.

After all, who will hire you if you don't have the right qualifications and experience to back yourself up during the interviews?

However, I have learned that there is another way to think about this.

Imagine being able to start any project, trying to develop any business plan, succeeding or failing and not being judged for it, because you're *young* anyway?

Being young and inexperienced is not something to perceive as bad. It's your golden ticket to *creating* things and making the experiences you need to make on the way, without judgements.

Nobody will remember you for the things you didn't succeed at, but only for the ones that you ended up being really good at.

This is your unfair advantage in your early 20s that nobody can use against you.

Being young means you have the freedom to try and be anything, gather experiences that will shape you, and use them as stepping stones to your dream career.

If you end up launching a project and being successful at it, you'll use it as a pivoting point in your career.

If not, guess what — you have just gathered an invaluable experience that will build your skills like nothing else will.

Chapter 2

Your First Business Job Glossary

Let me be honest with you.

Before writing this specific chapter, I found myself thinking that in the past 15 years of my life in which I have enjoyed the art of reading, I have never stumbled upon a business book going through the tools of networking or prospecting.

When I graduated from my Bachelor's degree, I knew that I wanted to major in sales and learn how to sell.

I did not necessarily know *what* I wanted to sell, or *where,* until I made my way into tech sales, but I soon realised that sales skills are transferable skills no matter in which industry you end up.

So, if you're out of a Business Degree soon, let me share with you a sneak peek of some skills and tools which you might be asked to use for your first job in business development.

And I had no idea they existed until my first day at work.

Most importantly, remember to leverage this knowledge at your next interview, to show that you have done your research.

Here are the *key concepts* I discovered as a junior business developer, during my first professional experience:

a. Prospecting

Your first business/sales job within a company will consist of helping the business to make more money. You can't put it more simply than that.

This often corresponds to an SDR (Sales Development Representative) role, which will require you to master the art of prospecting.

The simplest way you will be asked to generate money for the business is by booking meetings with potential clients that an Account Executive will lead to negotiation and then closure.

Your skills will help the company acquire new markets or expand in existing geographies.

In order to do so, you will need to learn about how to *prospect*. In other words, how to engage a first conversation with a potential client in a way that sparks enough interest from them to jump on a call — and move down the sales funnel as a potential opportunity.

The biggest eye-opener I learned when I started prospecting is that the message you are sending is not about you or the product you are selling. It's a genuine interest in the other person's/company's current situation or needs.

The best SDRs are the ones who believe in the product they are selling to the extent that they only push it forward when they see a fit with their prospect's need.

What helped me nail my first job as an SDR was spending time researching the companies I was targeting and the people I was speaking to, before pitching anything to them.

LinkedIn allowed me to reach out to a vast list of companies and establish a connection with its people, which then built the relationship.

To any future SDRs, remember to connect the product or service you are selling to a potential pain that your prospect is experiencing.

And to do so, the art of listening and asking the right questions will be the first skill to master.

b. Inbound vs Outbound

I couldn't believe how many terms I had learned in management or accounting that turned out to be useless in my first job.

So here is another key distinction you will hear on a daily basis in sales: outbound vs inbound.

An inbound lead or contact is an interested potential client who reaches out to you or to the marketing team directly, to learn about your offers.

An outbound lead is a contact that you reach out to after planning your territory and finding the right contact person, in order to engage a conversation.

Keep this in mind when you are applying for your first job, as some SDR roles tend to be outbound-only focused, while others might be a mix of inbound and outbound activities.

c. Territory Planning

This is another concept that you will need to master in your new business job and falls within the scope of organisation.

Let's put it as simply as I can: every sales team is assigned to a specific geography or territory in which they conduct prospecting activities.

As a matter of fact, if you are assigned to Southern Europe, your territory might include countries such as Spain, Italy, or France.

Once you have defined your region of focus with your manager, you will need to prepare a list of potential accounts (or companies) that might be a fit to the product or service you are selling.

The ability to plan your territory is a vital skill which will help you gain both time and credibility within your team.

I would advise that you should start by setting out a number of companies that you aim to reach out to, then putting together a file with their names, contact people, business information, and mostly the reasons why you think that there might be a fit.

This will help you segment your territory into A, B, or C priority companies, which will also structure your activity.

In other words, don't just reach out to anyone. Be strategic about it.

Plan your territory wisely.

d. Account Mapping

Similar to territory planning, account mapping is another organisational skill in sales which will make your life easier.

An account is simply a company name, or a group of companies in some cases, that are in your target contacts as an SDR.

Think of an account such as a company like Nestlé, Coca Cola, or P&G, for instance. Multinational accounts are often present within different territories, hence the importance of mapping your territory first before breaking down the account into different lines.

Mapping an account simply means defining in more detail within that company the department that you are aiming to get in contact with.

If you are selling a marketing solution, then marketing leadership is most likely the right fit.

If you are selling a product or service for their sales teams, then someone who's responsible for sales will be your target person.

For each account, break down the related department and find the right contact person title-wise before jumping into defining your personas.

The biggest tool currently used to identify these decision-makers is LinkedIn, as it allows you to go to the company page and find people through keyword searches.

e. Booking a Meeting

This all sounds great, but how do you actually book a meeting with a complete stranger that you have never spoken to before?

In my experience there are three effective and most common ways to outreach to a new prospect:

- **Cold calling:** Picking up the phone and calling your contact out of the blue might sound like a very aggressive method for booking a meeting, but if you do it right it does actually work.

The most important thing to remember about cold calling is that you need to be respectful of the other person's time by firstly introducing yourself, then asking them if this is a good time for calling, and if they can spare five minutes for you.

From that point onwards, it's extremely important to be as concise as possible about explaining who you are, what you do, and why you are calling them.

I would recommend mentioning things that are specific to their company and positioning yourself as a potential solution to that need you spotted.

An example could be: *"I am calling as I have had a look at your website and I can currently see that you are lacking xyz. From working with companies within your field, I can say that this has often lead to a xx% reduction in conversion rates. Would you be available to discuss this more in detail?"*

This could be an example of a conversation hack which allows you to open the door for additional time in their calendar for a discovery call.

- **Cold emailing:** This refers to sending personalised emails to your prospects. It's a technique that works just as well, as long as you aren't sending the same general emails through cadences. Prospects can very often spot when an email is part of a sequence and not personalised for them, so it is extrremely important to put extra care into your writing style. Emailing can also be a less aggressive way of establishing a first contact with a potential client.

- **LinkedIn:** Since LinkedIn started being the go-to professional network for companies, it has become easier to reach decision-makers.

The advantage of LinkedIn is that you can often learn more about the people you are targeting through their posts and content section, which allows you to establish a more personal connection.

In order to build a reputation on LinkedIn, you will need to invest in building your profile. And adding the right information for others to see your profile as valuable can facilitate interactions with them.

A good first LinkedIn message is the one that is not too intrusive, and can even start as a virtual coffee chat to learn more about the other person's role within their company.

People value human connection more than anything else, so make sure you are as natural as possible in doing so.

f. BANT

The first call you will book with a prospect is called a discovery call, where you will ask the right questions to understand if there is a fit between your offer and their need.

A discovery call can be very stressful when you are lacking structure, hence why BANT was created.

This is a sales assessment framework based on **Budget – Authority – Need – Timeline**, which summarises some of the important information you need to learn from this call.

Budget – although this is the first one mentioned, I would not advise starting the call by asking about their budget.

The ideal way to start a discovery call is breaking the ice by building a genuine connection, chatting about your background and learning about theirs, and trying to understand which challenge are they currently encountering in that specific area.

Questions such as: *"What is a top priority for you right now?"* or *"How does this priority affect the business and your role currently?"* will get you further than any pre-built pitch.

Budget is something that will very likely come at the end of the conversation, and a way to open up the topic would be asking them about their current available investment.

Authority, as the word says, refers to understanding if they are the decision-maker when it comes to the purchase or implementation.

Often, the person you are speaking to relies on other people's decisions, and involving most of them in the conversation early enough not only makes the deal progress faster, but also gives you access to different touch points in case some of your contacts leave the company or change duties.

Hence, ask and expand into the decision-making circle.

You can open up the topic by asking questions such as *"Are you the only person who is currently in charge of this project?"*

"Who participates in taking the final decision?" and asking to include those people in the next conversations.

Need refers to the current situation of the prospect you are speaking to.

There are generally two situations in which to assess a need: the one where the prospect is aware of the need itself, and the one where the prospect isn't.

Let me break that down into an example.

Imagine you are a shop selling photography equipment, and two clients come up to you.

One of them is complaining about the fact that his camera does not store enough photos, and he wants to change to another model with more storage.

The other one has the same issue, but instead of changing the whole camera, he is coming to buy a memory card in order to gain more storage.

The first costumer might be new to photography, and he does not know that you can spend less money by purchasing a memory card for the device instead of upgrading the whole camera into a more expensive device which might end up causing the same storage issue down the line.

Some might argue that the first costumer should have been aware that external memory cards exist.

But your job as a shop is to educate the costumer, not push him to spend money on a brand new device if he might come back later with the same issue.

That's how I define the job of a good SDR: understanding the situation and assessing the need where the costumer might lack knowledge, before proposing a solution that fits his use.

If you are able to assess the need in the right way, your solution will pretty much sell itself and fall into the context like the piece of a puzzle.

Listen to your prospect and ask about how the current context is affecting them, the business, and their financial results.

Then, gather the right data to show them how you can save them time, money, and effort in the process – through your valuable proposition.

Timeline refers to the timeframe in which the prospect would be ready to take a decision, sign the contract, and start the implementation process.

Assessing the timeline is extremely important for your company internally, as it allows you to coordinate things with the implementation team.

This also helps you set expectations with the client on their end.

In order to assess the timeline, you can ask questions such as: "When do you think you might be able to make a final decision?" Or "When would you ideally see the project starting/ending?"

Another important point to consider here is asking the client if there is anything urgent that might arise to speed up their timeline in the next weeks or months (such as a new product launch or pressure from the decision-makers), in order to give you the visibility needed on the project guidelines.

Besides these concepts, here are some cool *tools* I would advise learning about as well.

g. CRM (Client Relationship Management): this is a centralised place where all of your leads and conversations with prospects, outreach activities, and opportunities, will be tracked.

I like to think of the CRM as the brain of all sales activities.

A CRM can be any tool, such as **Hubspot** or **Salesforce**, which are some of the best known ones within this field. You will often be asked to save your activities on the CRM your company is using, which often has integrations to other tools and platforms such as LinkedIn.

h. Workflow platforms: A workflow platform is a tool that automates outreach activities such as email cadences, or helps you coordinate and keep track of your tasks in one place.

Salesloft is an example of a workflow platform which you might be asked to work with, and complements Salesforce in terms of efficiency.

It will allow you to set up automatised email cadences, keep track of your outreach, set up reminders for upcoming conversations, track your performance and progress, and will serve as a source of truth for further activities.

i. Data extraction tools: These are tools which your company might put at your disposition to help you find the relevant contact details of the people you want to reach out to.

Thanks to tools such as **Lusha**, **ZoomInfo,** and **Rocket Reach,** you can have a direct phone number or email of a potential prospect by extracting the information through LinkedIn. However, always check your company's legal policy before using such tools.

Two other tips that saved me from painful situations in my first job are the following:

Always ask if there is an NDA (Non disclosure agreement) in place before sharing sensitive information.

And make sure you log all of your activities, emails, and calls — everything.

You'll thank yourself later.

Chapter 3

Applying For Your First Job

Building your first CV

If you have had the experience of applying for an internship, a summer job, or a full-time position in the past, you have probably had to work on building your first Curriculum Vitae, or CV, already.

However, if you're one of the people who does not know where to start, or if you would simply like to know what has helped me in my career to build the kind of CV that lands you offers at top companies, I hope this section will be very valuable to you and dispel any concerns you might have.

The first thing to take into account when building your CV from scratch is to be at peace with the fact that this will be something which will be built up through the years.

I genuinely know that sometimes it can be overwhelming to read job offers where employers require several years of experience to get the job, but here is where you should start.

You need to understand that until you have relevant experience to put on it (if you already do, then that's great), your CV needs to be a combination of your interpersonal and professional skills, background education, and projects/led initiatives.

In other words, everything you did during your education years which will make you stand out from your peers.

CV structure example

These are the sections which your very first CV should duly include, and here are some tips on how to organise it.

Name/Surname
Optional picture
Date of birth or age
Current location
Phone number
Email address

Profile Outline*:

Employment History and/or Projects/led initiatives*

Educational background*

Extra-CV activities*

Languages Spoken

Additional Skills*

A profile outline* is a section to introduce yourself to the company in a couple of sentences. It should answer the following questions: *who you are, what you are known for, and what you are passionate about.*

An example of a profile outline could be: International Business student with a passion for B2B Sales and excellent relational skills.

A more experienced profile outline could be: Experienced Sales Professional with a proven track record of exceeding targets and increasing sales by building long-term relationships.

Your goal as a Business graduate will be to find a way to move from the first one to the last one by acquiring experience and developing your network, in order to build your credibility in the industry.

Employment History and/or Projects/led initiatives* is a section which will include your work experience to date – or in your case as a fresh graduate, any project you have worked on, initiative that you have led, or extra-scholar activities which you might have engaged in.

As your education history, this section must always list your achievements starting with the most recent one at the top, and then scrolling down backwards to less recent accomplishments.

This will allow the recruiter to have an overview of how your experiences have built you up to the role or position you have held most recently, but also to understand your progression path in chronological order.

A great trick to use when building this section of your CV is to mention the outcome of such experience instead of listing a succession of the tasks which were copied from the job description.

As a student, you could be focusing on your **accomplished initiatives**, such as follows:

December 2021 – March 2022, Master's degree delegate

- Served as the main point of contact between students and the Academy
- Coordinated class events with school associations
- Initiated a diversity council within the institution

Or:

December 2021-March 2022 – Project Lead, student initiative for company xyz

- Developed a go-to market strategy for company xyz
- Led a team of students to assess the company's expansion strategy
- Coordinated an outreach strategy with decision-makers in company xyz
- Forecasted company's initiatives for Q3 2022

As a more experienced professional, the main difference will be focused on backing up such facts with clear numbers of the outcome you created, especially if you're aiming for a Sales or Purchasing career.

In the future, this section of your CV might look like this:

December 2024 - March 2025 – Account Executive, Large Costumer Sales at company xyz

- Hit 200% of Q4 quota, an estimated €6.3M in pipeline
- Drove outreach, initial discovery & value-selling conversation across x accounts
- Closed deals in Retail, Manufacturing, and Pharma industries
- Supported enterprise deals in corporate accounts

Again, this gives you an idea of how this section should be organised.

Educational background: should include an overview of your academic studies, starting from the most recent one until the oldest one. I usually recommend mentioning any degree obtained after high school, as everything else goes too far back in time to be relevant.

- **MSc International Business** | Major in **Sales**, *London Business School*
  SEPTEMBER 2021 - SEPTEMBER 2023
    - Main areas of study: Economics, Accounting, Sales, Finance

  (Graduated with xyz honours)

This gives you an idea of how to structure your educational background, and also allows the person reading your CV to understand what you have majored in and studied beforehand.

Most of the time this won't necessarily be relevant to the job description, but it allows the company to grasp a first glance of your interests and background, to assess if you could be a great fit for the role.

Extra-CV activities: This section allows you to share with the recruiter what you enjoy doing outside your core role.

It's extremely important to be able to connect on a personal level as much as on a skills perspective, which is why I believe this is something to always think about.

However, this part does not need to be long; it can be a couple of bullet points about your passions. Sometimes it can also help you to bond during the interview stage, as the person in front of you might be passionate about the same things, too.

Languages spoken: I believe this section speaks for itself — do not hesitate to include the languages you master, besides rating yourself from beginner to native to give the recruiters some visibility of your fluency.

Additional Skills*: This section usually includes skills such as software mastery, specific programs, project management, but also any soft skills going from leadership to team management.

It's your chance to showcase your key abilities, and if possible to relate them to the position which you are applying for in order to show the recruiter why they should pick you.

Usually a CV should not be longer than one page, as it is often screened in a matter of seconds.

The key tip to use when drafting a CV is to adapt your skills and competencies as much as possible to the job you desire to get in order for the algorithm to recognize the fit between you and the position, if the CV is not screened manually by a recruiter.

This will also increase your chances of being selected and making it to the next round.

Once your CV is all set, a big part of your application is ready.

This document will allow you to apply to listed job vacancies on companies' websites, besides being able to be shared with recruiters who you might have direct contact with.

Pushing your application with LinkedIn

Now that you have mastered the theory, let's get into the practice and push your application into the 0.2% top candidates, in a couple steps.

I have previously mentioned **LinkedIn** as being one of the key tools which I use on a daily basis for networking and business purposes, but here is how to turn your LinkedIn profile into an interview generation machine (and I mean this).

If you're new on this social platform, there are two things I need to tell you in order to grasp your attention:

1. LinkedIn is the largest business-oriented networking website geared specifically towards professionals. It has over 500 million members, in over 200 countries.
2. 93% of recruiters use LinkedIn to research and recruit candidates.

This brings some relevance to why I believe it is necessary to not only build a good CV and start networking, but also to leverage your online presence to gain access to the right people.

What usually happens when someone applies for a job is that they will wait for the company's response, which might come into their inbox after a couple of days (or sometimes weeks, depending the size of the organisation) without taking a proactive initiative on it.

Once you have built your LinkedIn profile by following the simple steps which the platform asks you to follow (the same ones as mentioned in how to build a CV, but on LinkedIn sections), then add in a profile picture and you should be ready to go.

The first step is to set yourself as "open to work" from your profile section, in order to guarantee visibility to your profile while you are proactively seeking opportunities through networking.

The second step after applying for the position on the company website will be to hit the search bar button on

LinkedIn and type in "HR/company name" or "Talent Acquisition/company name" and filter the results according to your geography.

This will instantly give you access to a list of profiles from recruiters who are seeking candidates for that specific company in your selected region.

Now you should choose 2–3 of them and send a simple LinkedIn request, along with a personalised connection message, which states something like this:

"Hi X, My name is/your name and it would be a pleasure to connect. I have just applied for the position – link to the position – on /company name's/ website and thought I would reach out in order to know if you would be open for a call in this regard. Thank you, your name/"

Another alternative, in case no specific role is listed on the company's website that you can apply for, could be:

"Hi X, nice to connect! I thought I would reach out as I am currently exploring opportunities within the sales/HR/accounting industry, and /company name/ really grasps my interest. I would love to connect and speak further. Best, /your name/"

I know this is the kind of advice which might sound very silly, but it totally and undeniably works. It doesn't matter the company size, reputation, or current open roles.

Connecting with strategic people and showing proactive interest will push your application from no. 876 to no. 10

maximum, depending on the timeline when you take action and the personalisation of your message.

One thing which I believe is really critical to understand is that the job market is currently booming with open positions, which puts candidates in a very good spot, because companies are thirsty for talent.

The possibility to get into prestigious big companies is higher nowadays than it was a couple of years ago, due to the high selection standards and entry requirements which these businesses had.

You need to take advantage of this and leverage it for your own professional development.

By leveraging these soft skills, you have considerably higher chances of gaining access to very selective positions, just by getting directly acquainted with the person who might be in charge of the recruitment process.

The good news is that even if they are not the one in charge, they can still point you in the right direction or connect you with a colleague who is managing those open roles.

It's a win-win situation, and there is nothing to be lost.

And between you and me, worst case scenario – in case they do not get back to you after a couple of follow-ups – the list of recruiters is wide, so give it another shot somewhere else.

The process for landing your dream job or internship interview is based on a critical mindset shift, which comes from the understanding that you are a valuable addition to any company.

You would be *glad* to join this company as much as they would be *lucky* to have you.

Companies seek talent, and talent seeks growth.

If you are confident in your approach during your application process, and you know what you bring to the table and in which direction you would like to go, there is no reason why you should not get the job.

And I mean, any job.

Chapter 4

Acing Any Job Interview

The very first time I interviewed for a position, I was 17 years old and applying for a summer job, before moving out for college.

The position was to join the cleaning and meal prepping staff in a retirement house, not far from my parents' house.

On a human perspective, this was one of the most enriching experiences I had the chance to go through, besides working in the hospitality industry during the following two summers.

If I had to compare that interview to the ones I have recently gone through to land a job at Google, it would be like comparing day and night — completely different positions with different responsibilities.

However, there is something which I find to be pretty much similar when it comes to the psychological sides of human interactions in job interviews.

First of all, if you have never been through an interview and you are reading these lines, let's start at the very beginning.

A job interview is usually the first interaction which you will have with your potential future company, after submitting your application.

If you made it to the step where your CV is screened and selected, this is your time to meet a designated recruiter or an HR member from the company who will get to know you.

The purpose of an interview is for you and the company to assess if there is a match and a mutual interest to proceed further in the process.

And I put the accent again on *mutual* here, as many candidates tend to think that they are supposed to be only answering questions and hopefully be *liked* enough to make it further.

This is your chance to choose a company to which you will eventually be devoting your time, value, and efforts during the next couple of months or years. That means it's your time to ask questions and assess the fit, too.

There is a structure which I realised job interviews usually follow, and although the order of the questions might change sometimes, this is what the recruiter will aim to ask about during the call:

1. Your profile and experience based on your CV
2. Your reason for leaving your previous role (if applicable)
3. Your personality, key skills, and soft skills
4. Your leadership abilities, backed up by proven situations
5. Your technical knowledge and interest for the position
6. Your motivation to join the company
7. Your ambition of self-growth within the company

This is what will be assessed under the format of a conversation, and if you do your homework and put down the answers in a few bullet points, you will be more than fine.

However, and in order to help you answer such questions, let's break them down in a conversation with a recruiter and address each one.

1. Your profile and experience based on your CV

In this first part, you will be asked by the recruiter to introduce yourself in a couple of minutes.

This can be a tricky question, as you don't necessarily know which information you should filter or share because the question sounds a bit generic.

My advice here is to go for a quick introduction covering the following points: who you are, what you have studied/done recently, and what you are currently doing/seeking.

The best introductions are the ones that are short and sharp, but also express empathy. So don't hesitate to drop in a sentence about what you are passionate about, why you have decided to do what you are currently doing, or what led you to study business instead of biology.

Here is a template which you might like to use for it:

"Thank you for asking, and very nice to meet you. My name is X_ and I have graduated from X/ have been working in X for the past X years. I am extremely passionate about X, which has led me to study/work as X."

Depending on the recruiter, they will then ask you to go through your CV or give them an overview of your past experiences, too.

This will allow you to give them an educational/professional overview of what you have been working on during the past years.

So here is what you can use as a response:

"Of course, I would love to give you an overview of my experience. As you might have seen from my resume, I have graduated from X, with a major in X.

The reason why I have decided to pursue this field is because X, which has led me to specializing in X.

During my years as a student, I have been able to work on X and achieve X.

This has then led me to land an internship as X in X, where my main tasks focused on X and allowed me to achieve XYZ within the company.

My work experience as an X has also allowed me to master skills such as X and contribute to the company by XYZ."

A very useful tip to keep in mind when answering such questions is to follow the **STAR** methodology when sharing your experience.

Describing an event by following **Situation, Action, Result, Timeline** allows you to drive the recruiter through a chronological order of what you have been able to achieve through that experience.

2. Your reason to leave your previous role (if applicable)

This applies if you are in the process of interviewing although you are already employed.

It is often a tricky question which comes up in job interviews, where the recruiter is trying to understand why you are looking for a new challenge. They are also assessing if you are the kind of candidate who tends to jump from one role to the other without a clear strategy or plan in mind.

Spoiler alert: you don't want to give the impression that you are *that* candidate, no matter how lost you might currently feel in your job search.

Stay firm. Confidence is key when it comes to this point.

The question will usually go as follows:

"I can see on your CV that you have been employed in your current role for only X months. What is the reason you are looking for a new challenge right now?"

There is no perfect answer, but an idea could be that you are ready to embrace a new challenge and to acquire additional skills.

"The reason I am currently looking into a new role after my experience at X, is because I want to grow in experience and skills. My current job does not offer me a growth environment in which I can fulfil my maximum potential, which is why I would like to join your company as an X.

I am a very ambitious person who places self-growth as the top of my motivations, which leads me to seek a new dynamic environment."

3. Your personality and key skills

The most successful companies tend to hire for attitude and personality, instead of only focusing on hard skills.

In the moment when you're applying for your first job, you most likely do not have a lot of experience in the job market, which means that you will need to highlight your soft skills and personality more than anything else.

A **Soft skill** is defined as your ability to collaborate within a team, address problems, engage in conversations, deal with uncertainty, manage stress, adapt to a new environment, and so on.

These skills are what differentiates a smart worker who has the technical competencies to perform the job, from a brilliant worker who combines both technical and human skills.

And trust me, the difference is extremely noticeable from a mile.

The reason why soft skills are such an important factor in our society and in the current professional world, comes from the simple realisation that business revolves around people.

We work with people and buy from people, hence why customers are at the top of companies' priorities.

It's important that you know how to speak to them, build trust, and nurture long-term relationships. And this is something which can hardly be acquired if you only focus on the **Hard skills.**

Hard skills are competencies which you will acquire through experience, by working with specific methods or tools.

An example of a hard skill is mastering a specific computer program or understanding the fundamentals of project management.

These skills will allow you to bring more things to the table when it comes to industry knowledge or management style.

Soft skills are key skills which you will develop throughout your studies and working career, and which are becoming more and more valued in the workplace nowadays.

They include communication, leadership, team spirit, interpersonal abilities, and emotional intelligence, and they help you to collaborate better in the workplace.

Your interviewer will often test your skills by asking hypothetical or behavioural questions, which will put you in a situation where you need to explain which actions you would take from there.

Such role-related questions could be:

1. Imagine you are in charge of opening a new branch for the company in a specific country. Which key points would you consider before starting the project?
2. Imagine that your manager is out of the office, and a very important email that needs his approval has to be sent out to a major costumer by EOD. Which steps would you take?
3. Imagine that you are pitching a company's product to a customer for the first time. Which aspects would you focus on during the conversation?

These are generic questions which I have heard in my own experience, but there are plenty of variations.

However, the main goal is to test your ability to combine creative thinking, problem solving, and rationality, when making a decision.

There is often no wrong or right answer, as long as you are able to justify the logic behind it. And of course, as long as the reasoning is rational enough to make sense.

(PS. Sending important emails without any leadership approval, not considering a specific market, the company's goals, and the budget before opening a new branch, or pitching a product without even knowing what the costumer needs – they are all red flags. There is no right answer, though – hint.)

A good way to put your soft skills forward is to highlight how you are able to adapt quickly to a new environment, or how you excel at building trust-based relationships with those around you.

I am a true believer that 60% of succeeding at something is being a good human with healthy values and morals; the other 40% will require you to focus more on your skills.

4. Your leadership abilities, backed up by proven achievements

It's not about the experience – it's about what you make out of it.

One of my previous managers used to say that leadership is not given, it's proven.

And I couldn't agree more. Nobody will come to you and ask you to be a leader.

You'll need to prove yourself in many situations, and show the impact you have and the way you take accountability in specific circumstances.

The concept of leadership is a very interesting one, because the harder you focus on being a leader, the less successful you'll be at it.

But if you focus on the things you're doing and the actions you are driving, instead of focusing on the outcomes, things start to take a different turn.

One thing that will make you stand out in your professional career is the impact you are having on those around you.

Impact is a contagious thing. It tends to have a snowball effect once you've touched enough people.

The way impact is built is through resilience, a great ability to work on your own self, and aiming to help other people do the same.

I have met incredible people who have proven themselves to be successful, but with no track record.

No internal initiatives, no visibility. They limited themselves to being successful at the core tasks they were paid to do.

But in order to demonstrate leadership, you'll need to go beyond that.

Be successful at what the company's paying you to do, but don't limit yourself to that.

You can invest time in spotting a a problem that is happening internally, raise it up, and act upon it.

How is it specially affecting the team? How did you spot it? And mostly, how can you solve it?

Leadership is taking the lead on tasks that are completely out of your current role description.

A way to do that could be:

a. Spot the problem
b. Come up with a solution to solve it
c. Bring your plan to management
d. Offer to take the lead on it, and define clear expectations

e. Deliver on the plan
f. Use the STAR method to show how you solved a problem
g. Be vocal about it in the workspace

That's an outstanding formula to make sure that you're seen as someone who knows how to go the extra mile by keeping focus on your core responsibilities.

When a recruiter asks you to mention a situation where you have proven your leadership, there are mainly three things they want to know:

- What was the context?
- What did you do?
- What was the impact (if you can quantify this with a number or %, that's excellent; eg. I have built an internal document with all the necessary resources for new joiners, which shortened the learning cycle from 8 to 5 months)?

A simple framework to answer that would be:

In my previous position, I quickly realized that xyz wasn't working, and it was affecting our team by xyz.

I immediately spotted the issue and tried to think of ways that could solve the problem.

Once I came up with a plan, I highlighted this to my manager who was eager to let me work on this.

Once my plan was approved, we took action and documented the results.

My plan has helped to reduce/solve the problem by xyz (try to be number focused here).

It's all about the way you keep your own records, and how you use that to build your own self-narrative.

Remember, leadership combined with visibility are the perfect tools to elevate yourself and show that you're a doer.

Don't underestimate their power.

5. Your knowledge and interest for the position/position

This is one of the most important questions – the famous "why do you want this job?" question which you'll have to answer in most circumstances.

A recruiter's job is not only to make sure they match the right offer with the right candidate, but also to understand your interest and drive to join the company.

It's not really about motivation, as that fades away at some point.

There's excitement about jumping into the unknown, but there's also a ton of things which you won't know until you're 3, 5, 6 months in the job.

So, what they want to know is if you have the right profile (hard skills-wise) to apply for this job, and the right knowledge to build the ground for your core responsibilities.

They'll very likely ask you questions about tools or programs, if that's required in your job description.

But what will make the difference is the soft skills' questions part.

"What makes you a great candidate for this role?" or "Why should we choose you over someone else?" are not dangerous questions that doubt your worth compared to another candidate's.

They're simply a way for a recruiter to assess if you know what you bring to the table and how you explain it.

In other words, be self-confident yet humble.

Do not compare your skills to another potential candidate's skills in order to belittle them and show how you're "better", "smarter", "more successful".

Sit down, clear your mind, and think of past experiences you have dealt with and how they have built you and your character.

A potential answer could be something like:

"I have thought about it, after reading the requirements for this role, and most of those are things that I have learnt through my career.

I have had challenging times in my previous costumer-facing role, which has allowed me to build resilience, strong objection handling, and mostly a real drive to thrive in fast environments.

I know this role requires xyz attributes, and I am ready to bring those to the table.

Moreover, I did go through your company's mission and values, and I am happy to say that those are in full alignment with mine."

Not only will you be answering the question by making it experience-based and not ego-based, but you're showing that you have done your job in knowing what you are getting yourself into.

Candidates who show knowledge and research about their potential future employer can double their chances of getting the job.

And you don't need to know it all. Simply learning about the business and values of the company will place you in a really good position.

6. Your ambition of self-growth within the company

In the past, a company used to look for employees to fill up a position and perform specific tasks in their role. But that's not the case nowadays. Instead, companies hire for skills and potential.

Employees have changed, and so have employers.

Many of us want to work in an environment where we can thrive, grow, and feel comfortable enough to be ourselves.

An employee who is ambitious about his own self-growth is an employee that will perform at the best of their abilities in order to get the job done, make the company successful, and make himself successful.

A recruiter wants to hear you talk about your own growth plans within the role, what impact you aim to bring, and how far you want to go.

The best way to make a good impression when it comes to this is to ask questions about growth opportunities.

When the recruiter asks if you have more questions, do not back off and say that you don't.

Here are a couple of points you can bring up which will make you stand out from others:

- What is the growth progression for this role?
- What do people who have been in this role before tend to lean towards?
- What is the average promotion timeline for this role?
- What does the company offer to contribute to employees' growth?
- What degree of importance do training and career tools hold within the company?

Show the recruiter that you're excited to join the company, be successful, and grow yourself within the role.

This will show them that you're someone who is passionate, who values their own progression, and who's motivated by their own growth and not only by the title or the salary.

However, make sure you do make it clear that the role you are applying for will be your core and main focus until you have proven yourself to be successful in it.

You want to ensure that the recruiter understands that you're very career driven, but you're also someone who is reliable and will get the job done before going after the next piece of bread.

7. Explaining CV gaps

In our busy societies, most people will be afraid to take a sabbatical year or temporary step back from the professional world, due to the gap this will leave on their CV.

There is a general misconception that a blank space on your CV might be hard to explain in front of a recruiter, once you feel ready to get back to the job market.

Yet I genuinely believe that a *gap* becomes a *bad thing* only if you make it sound like it is.

There are tons of incredibly talented people who decide to step back from the workforce to invest time in their family, in their passion, or to travel the world.

All of these are extremely valuable experiences that can bring an immense amount of growth and self development, both personally and professionally.

If you find yourself in this situation, take a step back and acknowledge the experience you have gone through during the time you took for yourself.

Companies value skills such as creativity and self-reflection to a deeper extent, and often recruiters can be particularly impressed by a candidate who can showcase both technical and interpersonal skills.

If you think about it, most skills related to the business sphere, such as leadership, management, team collaboration, require a lot of interpersonal capabilities.

Being able to stand up for your values and embrace the experience you have gone through by sharing your learnings, can make you an even stronger fit for the role you are applying for.

I personally have friends who went to travel the world for some time and came back with so much openness towards new cultures and soft skills that they ended up in a higher position professionally speaking than the one they left.

Don't be afraid of your experiences; they are what makes you unique.

Use them to build your narrative.

Chapter 5

Getting Your First Job

Whenever we do something for the first time, we never know what is expected from us on the other side.

This applies to relationships, trips to a new destination, applying for a degree, or meeting with new people.

Landing your first job feels pretty much the same, fueled by the excitement and enthusiasm of starting something which will open room for growth and progress within your career.

The best advice I could give you here is to take your first experience as a discovery journey.

Once you have landed your first job, set up expectations for yourself but be open to embrace the learning experience. This will teach you so, so much.

When I first joined the business development team within my first full-time position, I was quickly amazed at the amount of things which were at the very core of Sales which I had no idea about — despite graduating with a Master's in Sales.

The advantage of graduating from a degree is the ability to address problems from a methodical perspective and to be very solution-oriented.

This has helped me to be extremely organised and strong on time management.

But everything else I have had to learn on the ground.

From how to write a great prospecting email, to how to pitch on a cold call without having people hang up the phone on you, to selling software to huge companies.

What happens when you shift from university to work is that you will very often lack specific guidelines.

The ability to learn how to prioritise the information, tasks, and initiatives will be a game-changer.

If you aim to start your professional career in the start-up environment, you will need to know that things can be very, very hectic, and often managers might expect a lot from you in a short time.

In walking through the discovery path that is your first job, you will need to find your rhythm, boundaries, and master two key things: being able to ask questions on things you do not understand, and saying no when you're at your full capacity in terms of workload.

Let's start with the first one — *asking questions.*

As with every discovery journey, you will be new on this ground, and depending on how lucky you get with your future managers, they might either understand that or directly expect things from you without necessarily guiding you.

I have stumbled upon good, less good, and not very good managers myself, and I can guarantee that it totally affects your experience within the company.

When you are joining a company, there will often be a lot of things going on, and everyone seems so busy trying to figure out the next project, training the next new joiner, onboarding the recent team member, or forecasting numbers for the next quarter.

But wherever you actually start your career, remember to take the time and give yourself the right to ask questions, request guidance if needed, and use the support resources which the company will put at your service.

Forget the fear of asking too many questions.

Being confused does not make you any less qualified than everyone else. You will need the time to go through the information and mostly give yourself the right to ask questions to get the respective answers.

The second one is — learn to say "no" when you can't take more responsibilities, and do not put more pressure on yourself by accepting every task just to look good in front of your managers.

I wish someone had explained this one to me earlier, because all I did initially was the very opposite. As a result, I often found myself in a position where I would be overwhelmed with the work because I had to deliver my promises.

There is only one thing worse than saying "no", and that is saying "yes" when you are not able to and carrying that weight on your shoulders.

The additional risk of always being the "yes" person is that some people might take advantage of it and put you in a very difficult situation.

They will start assigning you tasks which are outside of your responsibilities, including putting the weight of some of their own duties on your shoulders.

Be careful with this, and learn to distinguish the work which is yours to do from the rest.

Saying "no" doesn't have to sound negative. One way you could simply put it is:

"I would love to help on this one, but I already have xyz to do. Is there any of these tasks you would want me to delay, in case you require my help on this new task?"

And most of the time, they won't take the responsibility of you delaying anything.

Starting a new job is something everyone will experience at some point, for the very first time.

One of the biggest misconceptions we have as humans when getting into something new is the immediate pressure that we need to be good at it right from the beginning.

The standards might be high, and the expectations are there, but if you think you need to over-perform or leave no room for making mistakes, you're looking at things from the wrong perspective.

I will probably never emphasise this enough, but your first job is a true discovery journey.

You're joining a company for a position which might turn out to be interesting or not; you're in the process of discovering what you want to do.

You very likely have no idea about the variables that can influence your experience within the job, nor if you will find it enjoyable in the long run.

It would be unrealistic to feel as if you should have it all figured it out before even starting to learn. (Don't tell your interviewer you read this here. Actually, don't tell them I wrote this book.)

The trouble-saving tips

On the more practical side of any first job, there are three main things I have learned at my own expense and which I call the trouble-saving tips.

1. Make a copy of every document that is shared with you before editing it.
2. Always check there is an NDA (Non-disclosure agreement) in place before sharing anything externally.
3. Don't put the contact's email address in the email until you have finished drafting it, or it might send out before you finish.

If you consider these points, you're already further ahead than I was in my first job. And your manager will probably be delighted not having to go through this with you.

Nobody knows it all

One thing that I realised throughout my first work experience is that nobody knows everything.

This is something I live by today as well, and it's one of the most comforting and empowering thoughts that go through my mind.

You can be sitting with a colleague who has been in the company for years, and ask them about a specific product feature, and you'll probably have to find out the answer together.

I find that absolutely reassuring. And the reason for it is that we're living in a fast, change-oriented society.

If you're joining a software company, you'll very likely be faced with a product that goes through a trillion updates — constantly. It is humanly impossible to keep yourself up-to-date with all of them, besides memorising all of the essential features by heart.

So, my advice is to be curious and confident enough to know that nobody knows everything — but humble enough to acknowledge that you have everything to learn.

Knowledge & Systems

There are two core things that I would advise focusing on during the first couple months of your work experience.

Number one is product knowledge, and number two is understanding the systems.

The first one is self-explanatory, but I would still dig deeper into it.

Product knowledge does not only refer to grasping the details about the product, but also understanding which features you need to know about, which ones you need to understand, and which ones you'll need to explain.

This brings us back to point two — systems.

What I define as a system is an effective way of working which will allow you to structure your workload and save an incredible amount of time in the long run.

An example of a system is a centralised source of truth for any product-related questions, an excel spreadsheet of who your clients are and how you're approaching them (note this down on top of the three trouble-saving tips: document progress), and what are you planning to achieve there.

Systems include documents, spreadsheets, progress-tracking tools, forecasting tables, and anything you can use to maximise efficiency and sharpen your way of working.

If you're able to find a system that works for you, or – even better – build one, you'll gain an incredible amount of credibility, which will make you stand out as both organised and efficient.

Remember, companies hire people who are smart enough to do the job and hold themselves accountable for their own progress.

GRADUATE

Combining product knowledge and systems will give you a solid foundation into your way of working.

But as you might have grasped, that's not all.

Product knowledge and spreadsheets are only great if there is a strategy and a purpose associated to them.

When you're starting your first job, you'll probably be faced with prioritisation and time-management as being two of the core metrics on which your success will be based.

Most people think that the goal of starting a new position is to over-exceed expectations.

But you need to focus on learning how to do your job first.

Then you'll start getting better at doing your job with experience (through product knowledge, soft skills, and systems), and you'll start over-achieving and qualifying for a potential promotion.

Starting a job with the goal of over-achieving is like expecting yourself to rate the food before even arriving at the restaurant.

You can't take shortcuts when it comes to experience. You need to put in the work and wait for the results to come in. And, through consistency and the core belief that it will all make sense, everything will pay off in due time.

Keep in mind that the first couple of weeks you'll feel like you're starting school and everyone is already four or five semesters ahead — to say the least.

It will feel confusing and overwhelming, but the crazy thing is that any job will initially be confusing and overwhelming when you change companies.

Yet with professional experience also comes experience in managing the chaos and developing the confidence to know that as long as you put in the work, soak in the knowledge, and build your systems, you'll get through it.

Come with expectations

This one might sound almost surprising to some. Isn't the company supposed to be the one having expectations regarding you?

The answer is yes, but not only.

I have always envisioned a successful collaboration between two individuals as one where both parties have clear expectations.

Once you start your first job, just as any successful collaboration requires, I advise you to set your cards on the table.

Ask for the help you need, communicate about how you work best, and let your manager and colleagues know how they can support you to progress quickly.

There are so many young employees who join a company and try to adapt as much as possible without remembering that they need to also take into account their own wellbeing and way of doing things.

If you are in an environment where you feel respected, trusted, and heard, you will not only be more productive and efficient, but you will also be happier.

Numbers show that employees' wellbeing and evolution within their career path is one of the main reasons why retention rates can either skyrocket or drop.

People interact with people, and the companies that understand the importance of putting their employees first and creating a transparent environment, are the ones that are most likely to succeed and retain talent in the long run.

One way to set up expectations is by communicating your ways of working, such as putting together a short slide to share.

Include things that help your wellbeing, things that help you be more effective, how would you like to receive feedback, and how would you like your colleagues to support you (ex. 1–1 sessions, product knowledge decks, addressing projects together, attending your calls for shadowing, etc.).

Ask for feedback

Asking for feedback is one of the strongest assets on your table whenever you start a new job.

Don't assume that your way of doing things is always right, and always consider that there is a better way to do it.

Asking for feedback can be difficult, though, for two main reasons – either not knowing how to ask; or not knowing how to handle the answer.

The main thing is to ask for constructive feedback.

A constructive feedback framework would answer the following questions:

1. What is not working/can be improved?
2. How can it be improved?
3. Which resources can I rely on?
4. How should we track the progress?
5. What is the desired outcome?

The best feedback is the one which gives you enough room to both improve and measure the outcome of the improvement.

It's easier to track progress if you're starting from 0 and aiming for 5.

When you ask for feedback, it's important that the response provides you with a clear vision of what is expected from you and how the organisation can support you to get there.

When it comes to taking feedback… listen, there is only one way to put this.

If you are performing your job to the maximum of your potential, working and keeping track of things, then do not take negative feedback as a criticism of your own work.

It sometimes just means that there is a better and more efficient way to do things.

Be open for feedback and embrace it as an opportunity to grow, acquire more skills and knowledge, and do things in a more efficient way than the one you were using until then.

For your own knowledge, here are some ways to ask for feedback:

1. Could I pick your brain to ask for your advice on how I am leading this project?
2. I would love to hear your thoughts about how I am currently performing on this task and what could be improved.
3. I am always looking for ways to be more efficient in my way of working, so I could really use your insights on XYZ.

People like to be asked for their opinion and advice, as this assumes they're in a position where they are seen as an expert in the field.

And most of the time, they will gladly help and support you to get better at what you are doing.

Don't hesitate to schedule feedback sessions with your manager or your co-workers when you feel the need for it, and come to the meeting with a straight agenda (the five points listed above are a good starting point).

Feedback leads to progress, and you should aim for progress over perfection.

Chapter 6

Dealing With Uncertainty

When you are starting something new, you'll be dealing with a high level of uncertainty. That's a fact.

You can't possibly know what exactly is expected of you. But the first step of dealing with an uncertain situation is to recognise that you are facing one.

This might sound really obvious, but if you're putting pressure on yourself and not recognising that it is completely normal to not have a clue about what is going to happen, things might get trickier.

There is absolutely nothing wrong with walking into the office on your first day without any idea of what exactly you need to do, how the company makes money, or how you are going to figure out this or that.

The most important thing to remember in every situation where there is uncertainty is that you will get through it.

Train your mind to believe that you will figure this out, with experience and time.

You can't find shortcuts, and this is something I have learned from experience.

You need to go through the whole process, feel some stress and pressure, have moments where you feel like nothing is working… and then it will all click.

I can promise you it does, because we have all been there, or will be again, when starting a new experience.

Everyone is, was, or will be a beginner

I used to believe that people in leadership positions within my company had it easier, because "they certainly know how to do the job".

Until I had a chat with a VP who joined two weeks after me and didn't know what we were selling.

Then I understood that there is how to do the job, and how to do the job here.

Each company has its own specific rules, products, and ways of working. And no matter the level of experience that those around you have, everyone will feel, or have felt, like a beginner at some point.

So, be okay with not knowing things, and be okay with putting in the work and asking a ton – if not more – of questions.

They do not need to be elaborate, relevant, or technical.

There is no silly question, and people won't think you're stupid.

And no, you can't just skip the questions and let them pile up. I assure you, you'd rather not go there.

The most important thing you'll learn from uncertainty is how to navigate through it, and still find your own way.

This is one of the biggest skills you'll be able to use through your personal and professional life, and one of the most important traits to building confidence.

Put in the work, ask questions, and focus on systems and product knowledge: what are the things that need to be done, how to do them, and then, how to do them better.

Repeatedly, with the sole aim to improve.

Experience and time, combined with openness to feedback and a growth mindset, are your most valuable assets to succeeding in your career.

Be comfortable being uncomfortable

The best way to deal with uncertainty is simply by being comfortable with it.

One of the best pieces of advice I got in my career was "Be comfortable with being uncomfortable".

It's simple and plain advice, which does wonders for both your level of stress and your way of approaching the job.

Once you start understanding that nobody knows it all, and that what matters is your way of approaching things, you'll shift a big weight off of your shoulders.

It doesn't matter who you are speaking to, which problem you need to address, or how complicated a conversation could be, you'll simply master it by doing what is in your power at that specific moment.

I used to think that joining a company meant having a specific manual as a source of truth, that I needed to follow word by word.

In college, they require you to study your notes in order to answer exam questions. Mostly, because there's often only one right answer.

But school is not the reality, and there is no such thing as one way of doing things within a company.

To be fair, the companies which did stick to one way of doing things (have a look at Nokia or Motorola), did not really last long in the market.

You won't be handed a list of guidelines, and nobody will have the responsibility to make you aware of everything.

So you'll make mistakes, find yourself not knowing things, and it will be up to you to *go* and look for the information somewhere else.

And that will help you stand out more than anything else; your ability to be curious and proactive, and your resilience to make things happen.

My first weeks in my first job as a Business Developer were some of the most challenging of my career.

I simply had no idea about anything, and I felt like I was just there and things were going at an extremely fast pace without waiting for me to understand them.

It took me a bit of time before I understood the concept of self-accountability, and that nobody owed me anything.

If things went fast, they didn't have to slow down, so I needed to upgrade and find systems that would allow me to process the information faster.

And act upon it.

The seat becomes more comfortable when you have not been sitting on it for hours, and so does your work experience.

You need to figure things out before you can slow down and relax.

If you're taking initiatives, trying to find ways to make things work, and giving it your all, you'll eventually get there, and everything will start making sense one step at a time.

You can't blame it on everyone else, because the others are very likely too busy doing their own part.

Nobody can be held accountable, except yourself.

Never stop learning new ways

The most successful and smart co-workers I have met in my career are people who never stop learning new ways of doing the same thing.

During my experience working at Google, I quickly understood that good management is flexible management.

A great manager listens to each one of his team members and tries to learn about how they see, approach, and solve problems. He doesn't dictate.

His job is to coordinate, and support when needed, and that's the way I learned how to define Leadership.

When you develop leadership abilities, you'll learn to see the world from different perspectives and be excited about all the ones you still need to find out about.

If you're starting a new job, be open to conversations that will widen your knowledge and make you feel like there is still so much to grasp.

If your colleagues are doing things differently, be humble enough to learn from them and confident enough to share what is working for you.

As humans, we tend to operate and progress better when we communicate.

Make sure you keep a transparent and proactive attitude, and the growth potential becomes endless.

Collaborate with your team-mates

Collaboration is the key to success. The right companies, teams, and sales organisations will create an environment for their employees to thrive and to be transparent with each other.

We often think that working in sales should come with being extremely competitive and pushing yourself to be better than your peers.

However, the best success stories I have seen within the tech sales industry are from people who are not only great performers, but even better leaders. People who display collaboration and initiative to help others succeed just as much.

Imagine putting together multiple brains instead of only focusing on your own way of seeing things, and the possibilities become endless.

Being able to listen to other people's opinions, validate their way of seeing things, and encourage them to share their own thoughts, will not only benefit you in your daily job, but will assist the organisation at different levels.

Especially when you're contributing to creating the right environment for that to happen.

Never consider anything as obvious

Did you ever experience a situation so many times to the extent that you believed the outcome of it was just obvious?

You think you've been there before, so you know how it will go this time.

Thinking some things are just obvious brings your guard down and pushes your mind to operate through the same systems instead of exploring the situation from a different angle.

There is rarely such a thing in business as the same thing happening twice in the exact same way, and the sooner you look at every problem, project, and disagreement as an opportunity to learn how to cope with new mechanisms, you'll see the wider picture.

There is always something to be improved or considered.

So, approach situations with the goal of learning something out of them, instead of seeing problems as drawbacks.

Whenever you're confronted with a new opportunity to learn, embrace it and make sure you get the best out of it.

Detach from the outcome, focus on the inputs

Let me talk to you about a perspective my former manager at Google gave me that changed my approach to work.

Whenever you're working on a new project or trying to win a new client, there are two criteria to keep in mind: the things that are in your hands; and those that are outside of your control.

We often tend to assess and judge both equally, although their impact on the outcome is very different.

If you spend 90% of your energy on the impact you can make, and only 10% potentially wondering about what could go wrong, you'll very likely end up in a different place than someone who just stresses out about the whole thing.

My point is to not only focus on doing without analysing the overall environment. Just make sure you're not so obsessed about controlling everything that you miss some important steps on the way.

Be practical in the way you approach conversations and make sure everyone is on the same page, then do your best to make that a successful collaboration.

If you feel like you have done that, you'll have been successful at what you have been doing.

I had so many experiences where I gave things my best and sent over a deal that was due for signature the following day… then the business suddenly decided to stop any ongoing projects until further notice.

Disappointing ? Yes.

A failure where I can only blame myself and feel bad about it? Absolutely not.

Quantify and note the inputs, and they'll help you to explain the situation no matter the outcome.

When you learn to do so, you'll find it more easy to detach your own identity from the job you're doing.

Our careers take up a big part of our lives, and we tend to define ourselves by how successful or not we are at a job.

Sometimes, though, this can push things to the extreme, which is why it's important to remember that you're not your job, and your career is not a reflection of your overall skills.

A project gone wrong is a project where the client's needs didn't meet the offer in the current environment.

Emphasis on *the environment*, which you can't predict.

Make sure you keep yourself motivated enough that you don't let this draw you back, but only learn how to deal with similar situations better.

Equally, not every project can be qualified as successful from a financial perspective – or if we say it in another way, not every great deal results in an immediate flow of money into the company's finances.

Ideally, the sooner you bring revenue, the better you'll gain credibility as a sales person.

But some relationships are worth more than immediate cash flow, and if you learn to put the person's priorities before the deal itself, you might land on a goldmine.

You'll gain the client's trust as they'll see you as someone who wants their best interests, and at the same time you'll be paving the way for higher costumer retention.

And very often, the money will follow.

Become an expert or a go-to person

Everyone of us is good at something that someone else wishes they were good at.

We all have our own strengths and weaknesses.

Make sure you use your strengths in your favour, and become known for them.

Within every team, managers will quickly identify what each person masters best.

If there is something that comes easy to you – be it organisation skills, building Excel files, making catchy presentations, delivering concise pitches – practice that well, ask for feedback, then share your practices with the team.

Be vocal about your strengths, show your accomplishments, and talk about the things you did and how they drove change and challenged the status quo.

You will not only help folks who might have been struggling with these skills, but also gain your manager's recognition and be designated as the go-to person on a wider perspective within the organisation.

Showing with confidence the things you have been able to change, but also showcasing how you dealt with challenges within that specific project, will make you stand out.

And that will be an excellent way for you to gain visibility and practise your leadership skills, which will only benefit you and others in the pursuit of your next career step.

The most important thing to remember whenever you're leading a project as the go-to person is that your main goal is to serve others and benefit them, and not to only gain recognition for yourself.

If you do the job with the best intentions, the recognition will come to you.

Chapter 7

The Power of Self-Accountability

Networking is one of the oldest concepts of our society.

Before we even introduced money and currencies, people used to exchange goods they produced for something their neighbour produced or had in his possession.

In the early times, it was actually very uncommon to do any kind of business with a complete stranger, unless your relatives knew them or their family.

General opinion was what drove trust for such exchanges to happen, based on the reputation someone had.

That concept of reputation was the very beginning of what we call Networking today, thanks to the progressive access to education and opportunities.

As a result, most of us are the first or second generation in our family to attend university or obtain a degree.

We are conditioned to think that the golden way to success relies on obtaining a degree from a renowned institution, which will then guarantee us a stable career.

Yet we often forget to acknowledge that higher education might not be for everyone, and there are so many people out there who are doing *very well* without it.

Right now, whatever reason has led you to apply to university, I hope that you're excited to learn everything about the subjects you picked and absorb knowledge throughout the next few years.

But let me be totally honest, if your only motivation for going through university is to check a box on paper, I would probably advise you to do something better with your time.

On the other side of the spectrum, you won't be assessed on the degree itself but mostly on the person you became through the process, the skillsets you developed, and the impact you made and are aiming to make.

University does not make you smarter unless you're committed to becoming smarter.

I have met people who would come to class once every three weeks, miss deadlines, then magically complain that their grades were not going up or they were not learning anything.

The way that this usually goes is that these people blame it on the professor, or sometimes on the degree itself.

The university becomes questionable. The exams were too hard. The director of the programme didn't like them, that's why they could not pass.

The true reality behind it is that university is as useful and as interesting as you make it.

Self-Accountability will be your greatest power in navigating this journey.

Take away this idea from your mind that the school system owes you something, and that going through college will make you successful or guarantee you a great future.

Studying only makes you smarter if you use it as a means to achieve a goal, and to build your own definition of success.

That's exactly what university should be: a means on the way to your career, a possibility to absorb knowledge, to interact with smart people and learn from specialists about subjects that make you excited to learn.

I strongly believe that the value that something brings you should be measured by how much it is benefitting you as a person.

Ask yourself: who am I becoming through this experience?

Once you see every choice as a new learning opportunity to *grow* into a better version of yourself, you'll make more intentional decisions.

Let this be the beginning of this process.

Your grades only matter to a certain extent; your learnings will

We have often been conditioned throughout our childhood to think that to be *successful* in our careers, we need to excel and get the best grades in school.

Don't get me wrong, if you are going to school you might as well be successful in your exams.

But nobody talks about the misconception that this can create in a student's mind.

It's important to give your best in your education, but never attach your value or your level of intelligence to the outcome of an exam.

Focus on knowledge first, not on assessment.

Focus on performance, and not on results.

When you are passionate about something and you invest your time in it, your efforts and consistency will pay off and bring results.

But sometimes we are not necessarily motivated to excel in all subjects, and that's also alright – as long as you try your best.

Trying your best and figuring out that something is not for you is another way of being *successful*.

I have met many smart people at university who would be passionate about Business, fail an accounting class twice, and think that they would never be able to work in a company.

And that's just a total misconception.

You need to keep in mind that the classes you are taking are designed as a general set of learnings for different types of people, each one of whom has their own strengths and weaknesses.

Yet these lessons are delivered under one same specific format.

If you want to put it in a more philosophical way, what Einstein used to say was:

"Everybody is a genius. But if you judge a fish from its ability to climb a tree, it will live its whole life believing that it is stupid."

That's as logical as it gets. Your grades only matter to a certain extent; your learnings will.

But how do you make these general learnings matter then?

How do you make something out of them?

Don't settle for memorizing; absorb and expand your knowledge.

I came up with a general rule of thumb during my student years.

Whatever subject I would be studying or whichever class I would be taking, I would firstly focus on understanding it and then *expanding* my knowledge on it.

What I mean by expanding my knowledge is finding ways to relate these concepts to something that resonates with my perception, interests, and experience.

Whenever you are attending a class and absorbing the course's learnings, let your mind connect these concepts to things that interest you.

This will exponentially increase your understanding of it, but will also allow your brain to retain this information faster.

Here's an example:

When I applied for my Master's degree in International Business, I knew that there was one key learning I wanted to get out of it at the end of the two years:

How does a company make and manage money?

Every course I would attend would be directly connected to this specific end goal.

When I attended Accounting class, I knew that understanding a balance sheet and an income statement were lessons which I needed to grasp.

Sometimes, though, things wouldn't necessarily make sense after a class.

So, after revising my notes and reading the definitions, I would search for one or two resources on the topic that resonated with my curiosity and interest. This would be something like:

"How does a company's balance sheet reflect its financial situation?" or *"How to read a company's balance sheet"*.

I would then read about the stock market, deep dive into the concepts of assets and liabilities, and perhaps find an article that described similar topics through a specific practical scenario.

Sometimes understanding a concept becomes way simpler and more interesting when you see it from your own perspective.

Never let university become your only source of knowledge

If I could give my former self just one piece of advice, it would be to not simply rely on classes as my only source of knowledge.

Sometimes we are tempted to do this, as we spend most of our time studying for the subjects we have chosen and preparing for exams. But remember this: university does not give you the guarantee of landing your dream job.

It does not owe you anything when it comes to that.

The degree you are studying for is a means of getting there.

There is something extremely interesting about the choices that you can make during your student years and how much they can unconsciously completely shape your future career.

I mentioned that I pursued a Masters degree in Business, but let me tell you that my Bachelor degree was actually in Foreign Languages.

So how did I end up there? A series of events and choices I made along the way ended up taking me to the position where I am today.

During my last year of my Bachelor's degree, I was hired to work part-time at a professional event that lasted three days, and where I was in charge of welcoming Italian clients for a company – in Italian.

What happened during those three days shaped my entire vision of what I wanted to do, and how.

As I was in charge of costumers, I discovered for the first time what it was like to deal with the B2B environment.

I also observed how much speaking the language of the clients who were coming to see the company's products helped drastically.

There were three people on the whole stand: me, the CEO, and the CFO of the company.

And I was the only one speaking the consumer's language.

Then something clicked.

I remember walking through the event during my lunch break and speaking with other B2B companies.

Most of them were surprised that I could speak a bunch of languages and asked me for a business card so they could contact me in case they needed any interpreting/translation services.

I realised then that small companies in the B2C field lacked support when it came to translation and interpreting services for international events abroad.

It was often too expensive for them to hire a professional translator for such a short length of time.

What a great way to practise my skills and apply for a Master's in Business, after I majored in Languages!

I invested a couple of euros into professional business cards, a website, and started networking at business events within my city, and through LinkedIn.

I also knew that in order for me to dedicate my time to both studying and practising my skills with these companies, I needed to find a way to make this experience *count* as studying — which led me to applying for an Entrepreneurship degree, besides my Master's.

This allowed me to combine my practical degree and a theoretical one, have the privilege of not being obliged to take certain classes, and be able to focus my efforts on both my project and my degree.

It also gave me the opportunity to learn and practise business skills outside of the classroom.

Never let university become your only source of knowledge.

Through my own initiatives, I have been able to connect with incredible people during my studies, build solid business connections which I leveraged for my university internships, and learned a lot of things that helped me in my career.

This experience shaped my communication skills, contributed to building my mindset, and also made me stand out from the crowd for one simple reason: I did not let university become my only source of knowledge.

Whenever I needed to pitch myself in front of a recruiter, I had more to speak about than my Business degree.

And that is the power of the 1% that nobody speaks about.

Your network becomes your net worth

I can't stress this enough, and I wish I could write it so big that it fills the whole page.

Get out there and speak to people who have no connection to your interests and career path.

There is an insane amount of information available out there, and it's easily accessible to everyone.

When it comes to connecting with people, the value that technology has introduced into our lives is a huge asset to be used and leveraged for one's personal growth and success.

If you don't know where to start, let me give you a couple of ideas.

As a student, I used every occasion to attend business events, free training, virtual coffees, networking dinners, and any kind of event in the field of Entrepreneurship, to connect with people.

Websites such as **Eventbrite** and social media platforms such as **LinkedIn** allowed me to build priceless connections in my early twenties – and still do.

The importance of networking in business is so important to the extent that one connection can directly change the course of your career forever — whether that's through knowledge, circumstances, or position.

Be bold and curious enough to put yourself out there and meet new people, ask questions about their background and feel comfortable discovering things about new industries, trends, and positions.

But most of all, make sure that every person you meet remembers you for the values, attitude, and personality you radiate when you share a conversation with them.

If you can make sure they keep a good memory of you, you're making a priceless long-term investment which can hugely pay back in the next years of your career.

In the first year of my Master's degree, an American-based company reached out to ask me to fly to an event in Portland, to help them with translation for their French clients.

Absolutely insane.

That's what I thought when I opened the invite email in my college room after coming back from a long day of class.

This company was trusting me enough to pay for my trip to the other side of the world, to work with me.

It transpired that a CEO from a company I had spoken with during the three-day event I worked at, had referred me to them.

The connections you build with people might be your golden ticket to a new succession of adventures and experiences.

If you're just starting out in university, or are finishing your last year, use this time to be as creative as you can.

Try things out.

There will never be a better time than right now to test, create, share, connect, and implement new things.

And once you plant the seeds, just sit back, relax — and enjoy the snowball effect.

Chapter 8

The Power of Mindset

Hold yourself accountable

I have always been a passionate minimalist.

I love putting attention into details, spending time putting a dish together before eating it, decorating my pancakes with fruits in a way that looks enjoyable before I taste them.

Keeping my place organised and extremely clean, allocating objects into a specific spot in the house.

Some, like my mum, would call people like me obsessed.

But with my way of doing things, I grew to learn that how you do one thing is how you do everything.

The space in which you live reflects the way your brain is operating.

If keeping your surroundings clean helps you to be more calm and organised, do it every single day.

Small things like that and creating non-negotiable habits, such as exercising, are a great way to build structure into your day and hold yourself accountable.

Self-accountability is your most powerful asset in a world where everyone blames their pain on the circumstances.

People are often inspired by those who hold themselves accountable and stay on track: in fitness, at work, in business, in relationships, in the way they communicate with others.

The small habits and boundaries you set yourself and others will reflect your ambition and discipline in life, simply because the way you do one thing is often the way you'll do everything else.

If you only put energy into the things you *want* to do, the things you hate doing will probably catch you later.

Pay attention to how you do the small things, because they add up into huge, big ones, and before you know it they reflect your reality on a daily basis.

If we don't pay attention to the intentions we are setting daily, we will very likely end up at a destination we were not aiming for.

The purpose of this chapter is to teach ourselves the habit of paying attention to the way we process things, think, and act, in specific circumstances.

Not just in life, but also when it comes to our professional goals.

Initially I struggled to understand the concept of intention-setting and long-term planning.

Set your priorities first

When you're applying for a job, stepping back from your current position or changing careers, it is important to keep one thing in mind.

A job is an add-on to your life that will give you the opportunity to develop certain skills, make an impact in society, and gain a financial reward from it which will support your needs and ambitions.

A job's purpose is to serve you, in the same way that you are supposed to serve the company for the role you are fulfilling.

What I mean by that is, it's important to set the direction in which you want to go and think about your non-negotiable terms.

If you value flexibility and working on your own hours, you might accept a role that pays a lower salary but gives you that perk.

If your ambition is to make more money without worrying about the time you'll need to put in, your criteria will be different.

There is no better or smarter choice; everything in life comes with its own conditions and price to pay.

It's up to us to choose the circumstances that fulfill our own expectations.

So, ask yourself in which direction you would like to go.

Find a purpose in the things you wake up to do everyday.

By doing so, you'll be able to build the trajectory of your own professional life and not wake up everyday feeling lost or hopeless.

One of the biggest strengths I have built during my journey from being a college student to entering the workplace, is the ability to follow my intuition and constantly question the direction in which I am heading.

If you ask some of my friends, they'll probably tell you that I am an over-thinker who asks a lot of questions and needs to have a clear vision of the picture before taking a step in a specific direction.

If you ask me, I am someone who likes to know what I am getting myself into and who measures the correlation between my expectations and the opportunities I am confronted with.

Asking yourself the right questions and being honest about where it will lead you if you neglect your own needs and non-negotiable terms, is an excellent formula for mitigating the chances of disaster.

It also helps to build self-confidence and clarity about where you want to get to.

Here is a **checklist** I have created for myself over the past couple of years to make sure I am considering my personal wellbeing whenever I contemplate working with a company.

1. Does this company's culture align with my values?
2. What value can I bring to the workplace daily?
3. What is my potential evolution within this role, and what's a realistic timeline for that to happen?

4. Does this position meet my current professional goals?

5. Am I being paid at least the average market wage for this position within my region?

6. Does this job allow me to keep working on my own goals on the side?

7. How does this job support my personal life?

Whether I receive a job offer from a company or decide to work on a project with a client, I'll make sure I go through these questions as a guideline.

Don't hesitate to bring some of them to your interview with the company. Recruiters value candidates who are brave enough to ask questions about how the company can support their journey.

If you're bold enough to ask the questions, you will very likely get the right answers and then be able to make informed decisions instead of just hoping for the best.

First impressions last

When you're starting a new role, you will also need to keep in mind that first impressions of you are often what people keep for the longest time.

If you fail to deliver on your first project with your manager or fail to meet your first deadline, it won't go unnoticed.

And unfortunately, people might tend to assume that you will replicate every single project in the same way, so they will fail to trust your work.

Unless, of course, you're able to justify why you didn't deliver according to your manager's expectations.

At work, people tend to assume that how you do one thing is also how you do everything else.

If you can show them that you're able to lead a project with confidence and take accountability for the different steps, you will be seen as someone who knows what they are doing.

You will be trusted with bigger responsibilities. And if you use this opportunity wisely, you will soon be able to stand out from the crowd.

In order to be perceived as someone who does things effectively, you will need to deserve your spot fairly and show that you're able to deliver according to expectations.

This is a tricky one, though, as you'll need to make sure you're not constantly over-delivering at the beginning. Remember, first impressions matter just as much when you're on the opposite side of the road.

If you're initially putting in too much work, once you decide to slow down to your normal pace you might be perceived as someone who doesn't keep their promises.

So, it's important to find your balance and be smart about how you showcase yourself and your skills.

Make integrity your currency

A key factor when you're getting started with any company is to make sure you invest time and attention in the way you interact with your colleagues.

People are curious to know who the new recruit is, and most people will even be excited about helping you to settle down. Others, however, might not be.

Some might want you to be fired without you having any idea about it.

Don't take it personally.

Whatever their intentions, you need to be smart about how you address things, issues, people, and confrontations.

I was recently speaking to a friend of mine who started a new job in a consulting company, and got fired within two months.

I was surprised to hear that, because she's one of the smartest people I have ever met.

It turns out she had shared a feedback on her manager with one of her colleagues, who made sure the boss knew about it before the end of her probation period.

You never know what the person around you is thinking about, so be kind and eager to help… but be professionally smart.

Set boundaries and make yourself respected by having excellent behaviour.

It's hard to build a new reputation as someone who is honest once you have made a mistake that involves someone else within the company.

And the first impression you'll leave within your workplace will certainly follow you, so always be careful about what you share and who you share it with.

Your reputation is your highest asset in your professional career. Treat it as such.

Set realistic expectations for yourself

After finishing university, most of us tend to set the bar very high, which is great until you start doubting yourself and thinking you're not good enough because you didn't get that job at McKinsey at your first time of applying.

Your first job does not define the greatness of your skills, and your first experience after college won't most likely pay you six figures per year.

If you're a fresh graduate from a Business degree with a couple of internships as professional experience and no idea of how Sales or Purchasing really work in the practical life, you're starting from the beginning… as everyone does.

However, it's extremely important to understand that your own realistic expectations about yourself are what will drive you to achieve, believe, and do more in order to match your aspirations.

Yet, the key words to keep in mind here are: be patient while planting the seeds, but be smart to notice when the tree is not really growing.

When I joined my first company for a full-time position in Business Development after completing my degree, I was initially supposed to be an intern for the first six months.

Once the internship was completed, the company would assess if I was good enough to be offered a full-time position within the team.

However, the expectations which I had for myself were different, and I aspired to getting a job with them from the first day, without going through the internship phase as obviously there was less compensation.

When I attended my first interview with the recruiter after applying for the internship position on the website, I went through the whole process and spoke about myself and my early achievements, then I shared my expectations.

This is pretty much how the conversation went:

"In terms of position requirements, there are a couple things which I would like to suggest, if you might allow. I have previously gained experience in Business Development, by doing abc and engaging with costumers to help them achieve xyz. I do understand that your company is offering an internship position for Business Development which I did apply for, but I truly believe that by joining your team as a full-time employee, I would be able to bring the most valuable contribution in terms of business outcome. Would you be open to considering that?"

Now, that's not a script to follow by heart, but what I am sharing with you is how I aligned my expectations with the company's goals.

Their goal as a business was to expand in new markets and acquire new clients. I had experience in doing this and

GRADUATE

I could speak a couple of languages, which would help tremendously.

We both had something to gain from each other, so I asked for what I expected for my own growth within the company, and that did not include an internship.

And they said yes, and opened a new role for me.

Surprisingly enough, a couple of months after joining the team as a full-time employee, I discovered that I was the most junior one in terms of practical experience, but I was being paid more than some of my colleagues.

I went from applying for an internship to opening a job position within the company which I automatically filled myself, convincing the VP of Sales to let me work on a wider region in terms of outreach coverage, and earned a very decent entry salary for a should-have-been intern.

There is no limit to what you can achieve when you set up realistic expectations and back them up with facts.

If I had not gained insights on business development, even slightly – by being proactive during college – I would have not had anything to back up my words, and my credibility would have not been as strong at that time.

I was speaking about salaries with a former classmate at that same time, and she was earning less than half of what I was, by being an intern in a company which considered her as too unexperienced to join as a full-time employee before those six months.

Same school, same degree, both graduated with good grades — different expectations backed up with different facts.

Different results.

Do not be scared of asking for what you deserve

It's your time to shine.

If you're graduating from a Business degree right now, you're joining one of the most fast-paced markets when it comes to filling business and sales positions.

The industry has been booming since the pandemic started, and most companies have grown exponentially by cutting their costs on on-site initiatives and are recruiting *more than ever.*

If you're out of school and applying for your first job, do not be scared to ask for what you think you deserve, and back it up with facts.

Companies are spending an insane amount of money on recruiters in order to find top talent, and an equivalent insane of money into their employees' wellbeing to make sure that they do not leave for a better opportunity.

Honestly, I have worked for companies that offered crazy and amazing benefits for their employees: trips to private islands in private jets; an unlimited gym and sauna membership; training programmes; food delivery budgets; Uber rides for free; crazy bonuses for helping them hire new people, and more.

The point is, they have money to spend.

If you're starting your career and you know what you bring to the table, do not be scared to ask for that salary rise you had in mind — but remember, you have to back it up with facts.

If a company understands your worth, skills, and your plans in terms of growth with them, why would they not pay you more instead of keeping the hunt going for someone to fill that position?

Most companies cannot afford to let great people go, so make that your power to negotiate something out of it.

And if you can, ask for stock options.

Your first job will be a great experience that will help you determine what you want and what you'd like to do next.

However, as with every first experience, it won't be permanent. And it will be up to you to decide when it's time to leave.

Your first decision is not your final destination

Before joining a company, I always had in mind that this first job had to be it. I had to like it so much that I would stay with the company for the longest time.

Obviously, thoughts and expectations change when you're put in specific circumstances, and that's what I would like you to learn here.

You never know if your first relationship, your first job, your first business idea is the right one, until you try it out and experience it.

This is vital to keep in mind, as we often tend to set very high expectations from situations which we clearly do not know yet, and where things might play out in a completely different way.

When you're joining your first post-studies job, keep that in mind and embrace the experience as a possibility for growth and development, without pressuring yourself under unrealistic standards.

As you continue walking the path of growth and accumulating life experiences, you will figure out how important it is both in life and business to master the art of being present in the moment.

It's mind-blowing how things are more enjoyable when you take them as experiences and detach yourself from the outcome.

It's a key learning to understand that most events you will go through will be defined by two factors: things which you can control; and events which happen out of your control.

Focus on taking decisions that make sense for you, and give your best but never try to anticipate anything or control the outcome, or try to deviate the course of those things when they are not under your control.

If I had read this somewhere a couple of years ago, there are some things which I would have surely handled through a different perspective.

So, this is my advice to you: take the decisions that make you happy, and mostly that make sense to you.

Do not try to control the outcome, but give it your best shot to make the most out of everything.

Do not let people pressure you

When you're starting this new chapter of your life, you might find yourself being pressured by your close circle, which can be your own family, close friends, or relatives.

Hearing sentences such as "So what are you doing now?" or "How are you going to use your degree?" can sometimes be a heavy statement to respond to, for the simple reason that you most likely have no idea. And that's totally alright.

We often tend to project our own expectations on other people, forgetting that everyone is walking their own path.

I personally have friends who decided to leave everything behind for one year and explore the world after graduating, while others launched their own company and went fully into entrepreneurship.

Can you guess who turned out to be happier?

No, because both did, as they are living up to their own expectations, decisions, and standards.

And it is often forgotten that everyone should do what sounds like the best choice for them.

When you're dealing with close relatives who are already impatiently asking about your next steps, next source of income, life decisions, and status of your professional life, understand that you have the right to not give them an answer.

In the most polite way possible, let them know that you're taking your time to work things out and find what makes you happy before taking a decision.

And when you take one, know that you're also allowed to not communicate it immediately and to share information in your own timeline.

The ability to hold yourself accountable for your decisions and set healthy boundaries with your loved ones will make your life easier.

And a quick one for the win: if you can keep the frequent "so, how much are you making?" answer to yourself, you might thank yourself later.

What I would like to convey through my words is that whatever you decide to do, do it as long as it makes sense to *you*.

However, if making your own way in the business world is what sets your soul on fire, then I am happy to be sharing my own experience and walking that journey with you for as much time as you keep this book with you.

Hold yourself accountable for your own decisions

"I believe that accountability is the basis of all meaningful human achievement." – Sam Silverstein

GRADUATE

You read that right.

If Silverstein defines accountability as the basis of all human achievement, then it is definitely worth understanding it and holding yourself accountable for your own initiatives.

The ability to hold yourself accountable simply means that you make your decisions by yourself and take responsibility for the consequences.

Do not get me wrong here, asking for advice is often a great way to gain insights before choosing your next step. But my advice is: take all advice exactly as it is – advice.

Only act upon your own considerations of the situation when making a decision, as you're the only person who is completely aware of your own feelings and circumstances.

The reason why Silverstein defined accountability as the basis of human achievement is simply because most likely two things will happen when you're making a decision: it will either be a good-to-very-great decision which will make you happy, or a not-very-good-to-bad decision which you will need to get over.

In both scenarios, the ability to only hold yourself accountable for the outcome is the greatest power of mankind.

This will allow you to celebrate both your successes and losses as being a consequence of your own decisions, but mostly – and most importantly – to live in harmony with others and not blame them for your own fate.

The skill of living your own life in a way which does not blame circumstances on external events, but takes into consideration your own judgement as the starting point, is a gem that most human beings only master very late in life.

It is purely the start of where you take action and understand that you can achieve whatever you set your mind to achieve, as that's where it all begins.

Always keep this in mind and go for the path which makes the most sense to you at that specific time.

Another key factor to master here is the ability to understand that what makes sense to you right now might not make the most sense when you look back in a couple of years' time.

And that is totally okay. Disagreeing with your own previous decisions is the first sign of progress and growth.

The past version of yourself didn't have the insights and knowledge that your current version does.

You have time, make it count

When you're starting your first job, you will suddenly feel like you need to figure everything out at that specific moment.

It's a hard situation to find yourself in, and it's a lot of pressure on your shoulders to believe that you need to have it all figured out immediately.

Your early twenties are considered to be the best time for exploring, testing, and discovering what you would like to do next.

GRADUATE

I have walked through the same path myself, and I know that sometimes the transition to the professional world can be hectic, heavy, and overwhelming.

What happens after university is that everyone starts expecting a lot from you, without directly letting you know that you're a grown up now – and you need to work this out, right now.

The power of understanding that your life must flow within your own timing, without being burdened by other people's projections and expectations, will set you apart from everyone else.

However, this is only a result which you can aim to achieve when you become confident enough to know that you are the only one to be held accountable for your decisions, and more importantly, that whatever happens you will make it work out to achieve the best outcome.

I have a younger sister who is currently 19 years old and is walking her way into the college life, but is already starting out with an unfair advantage.

She knows very well that she wants to be successful, but she hasn't figured out how or what she will do to get there.

However, through my own journey, my parents have experienced in advance that it is better to not expect anything from your children for them to be successful on their own.

Whatever judgment, fear, opinion, or statement she might have on her journey, must stay where it is unless it's communicated to her as advice.

When you put yourself in a position where other people cannot influence your decisions, you're in a very powerful spot and you can focus on making the very best outcome out of your circumstances.

Moreover, you learn to hold yourself accountable for your journey and build a very strong relationship with the most influential person in your life – yourself.

Focus on your own growth; comparison kills progress

One of the key things to keep in mind when leaving university is that the people around you will also be moving at their own pace and achieving some things before, after, or at the same time as you are.

This is what constantly happens in life, and what you'll find yourself being part of in every environment.

Maybe you applied for a job at the same company and they got in but you did not, or maybe they did not even apply but a recruiter reached out to them, and not to you.

That's life, and you need to let go of the feeling of constant comparison to your peers, and learn to be genuinely and undoubtedly happy for their success in their own timing.

The ability to focus on your own growth, improving and developing into the best version of yourself, will not only save you time and bad feelings but most likely inspire those around you and attract great things on your way.

It is often easy to fall into the trap of comparison, and sometimes those who love us most can initiate it by mentioning someone else's achievements or comparing us to another person, without necessarily wishing to upset us.

You need to learn to let it go and respond with enough maturity and confidence that you are walking your own path.

And it will never be a perfect path, I can guarantee you that.

It doesn't matter how green the grass looks on the other side, how financially independent someone is or how successful that person became, you'd rather walk your own path – trust me.

So, don't dig deeper or feel in competition.

I am a strong believer that wanting the best for those around you allows you to be a person of values but also pays back with interest.

Several times I have had the chance to do a friend a favour by referring them to a company with which I had a close connection, or stepping back to let them take a job which was not right for me at that specific time.

The way this strengthened our relationship is more valuable to me than any potential source of comparison in the first place.

"The only one you should compare yourself to is you. Your mission is to become better today than you were yesterday. You do that by focusing on what you can do today to improve and grow."

– John Maxwell

This is one of my favourite quotes from Maxwell, which highlights that your only source of comparison should be the previous version of yourself.

From there, you should only aim to get better.

Don't stop moving

This one is for all of the times you might apply for a specific internship, job, or company, and find yourself facing a rejection.

I know that it can be hard, demotivating, and not rewarding for all the effort that you made to graduate.

The way I have gone through this myself is to keep moving.

Imagine a golf ball. As long as it's moving towards the hole, the chances of it getting there are higher than if it stopped after a couple of seconds away from it.

It might sound like a very simplistic analogy, but to be completely honest this small metaphor has led me to stay consistent more times than you could ever imagine.

Whatever the outcome, focus on the movement and you will end up achieving your desired result.

It's important to understand that whenever an application gets rejected, or your resume does not receive a positive feedback, the best way to use this experience is by trying to understand what can be improved.

Some often say that rejection is just redirection, and this is something which I firmly believe in, too.

We all had, or will have, times when something which we wanted so, so badly ended up not working out – only for us to realise at a later stage that this was the biggest blessing.

And often, you probably found yourself ending up in a much better place than you initially thought you'd be.

The road from being a student to becoming a full-time employee is sometimes not as smooth as you had expected it to be.

But you need to give yourself credit for trying, and to be confident that things will turn out in the best way possible for you, at the right time.

Your most valuable asset in doing so will be your mindset and the way you approach whatever circumstances that life throws at you.

Do it with the conviction that you're on the right path for you, walking towards your own goals.

Leave your comfort zone

As I am writing these lines, I am thinking of the first time I left my comfort zone and pushed myself to pursue a dream, an ambition, or a goal that I had.

The truth is that I had never been taught to jump into the unknown, travel by myself, or relocate countries for a job.

I have always felt extremely grateful and blessed for growing up with the possibility to make my own choices and pursue my dreams, which pushed me to become extremely independent from a young age.

I wanted to succeed so badly that the only possible direction was going forward, and figuring things out on the way. And it made me understand the importance of setting a *Why* behind every goal.

Whatever you decide to pursue in life, I believe that it is extremely important to define a *Why* for yourself.

Your *Why* will be the reason you'll be pushing yourself to go the extra mile, or to stay awake later to work on a dream you only believe in, or to make yourself go to the gym when you don't feel like it. And the *Why* can be different for each one of us.

The reason that I mention this is that once you have defined your main *Why*, everything that is needed to get there will only be an additional step.

But sometimes these steps will require you to jump out of your comfort zone and try something new, and I want you to embrace these new beginnings as a possibility for growth.

No matter how scary it might initially sound.

The first time I travelled by myself on a plane, I was 18 years old and flying to London for a whole weekend. I had grown up dreaming of visiting that city, but had always been both scared and hesitant about flying somewhere alone, and being far from home by myself.

GRADUATE

A couple of years later, I moved to London for an internship, and the next year I was flying to Portland (USA) for a longer time.

A continent away from home and an eight-hour time zone difference on the clock.

Now, I have relocated countries for work several times, by myself.

The secret here is to take small steps towards what today might sound impossible.

Every milestone in life can be achieved when it is broken down into smaller steps.

Remember that whatever you set your mind to, as long as you *don't stop moving* in that direction, you'll end up there.

Chapter 9

Focusing On What Matters

Making the right choices

As humans, we are the only creatures that are given the concept of choice over our lives and circumstances.

If you think about it, it's fascinating how every moment is a consequence of a choice we have made or refused to make.

Every day we wake up to the possibility of making decisions that will determine how the next days will unfold.

The most important decisions you will make in your life will need you to be focused.

And the ability to focus on the things that matter to you more than anything else will simplify your decision-making process in ways you couldn't imagine.

Whenever you're facing a situation where the choice seems difficult to make, think about what it is going to cost you (and I am not talking money-wise) to go in one direction instead of another.

Ask yourself what things you would need to sacrifice and whether you are eager to trade some of those for something else.

Whatever path you decide to take in life, or in your professional journey, my greatest advice to you is to always keep your priorities in mind.

When I first started my journey into the professional world, I was extremely excited about learning as much as I could, and I was ready to work as hard as I could to reach my goals.

To land my "dream job".

Whatever that meant, I didn't take the time to define precisely what I was aiming for and what I was not willing to trade for it to happen.

Fast forward a couple of years, I had changed jobs four times in three years.

It's a funny thing how our brains tend to idealise our perception of the external world, especially when it's related to something we don't have and we're working for.

Something we're aiming so hard to get.

It took me time to discover that there is no dream job out there.

But there is surely a job that will fulfill your expectations – once you have set them.

Define your own vision of success

We often tend to start something without knowing what we're getting ourselves into, and are then disappointed once it turns out to be different than the way we had idealised it.

But nobody ever promised it was going to be *that* way.

Yet we tend to believe our fantasies, trust other people's perceptions, and seek external validation.

Think that every journey is the same.

Judge ourselves on other people's accomplishments.

Compare two outcomes based on completely different paths.

Your ambitions through life will constantly change and evolve, and so will your thoughts about your professional career.

You should constantly question if your job aligns with your priorities and long-term plans. And if not, be selfish and practical enough to explore other possibilities.

The simple act of keeping in mind the things that truly matter to you, and updating this list as they change, will save you from a huge amount of time overthinking the decisions you make.

It's hard to keep track of our own priorities in a society where things tend to move fast and everyone seems to be working as hard as they can for their next promotion or financial achievement.

And there's nothing wrong with doing so. But understand that your priorities might be *different*.

I used to think that working extra hours and over-delivering was my secret weapon to success. Then I discovered that I had no real interest in being promoted faster if I had to trade my personal time and wellbeing for it.

There's no rush in life; everyone walks through it at their own pace, and mostly, guided by their own priorities.

Some people might be okay with staying at work until late, others will be okay with working normal hours and leaving earlier to pursue that side passion they have.

And funnily enough, you might even find out that both people have delivered the same quantifiable value to the company on a work day, because people work differently and at a non-comparable speed.

So, don't judge yourself on someone else's definition of success. Understand that you should aim to create your own.

The perfect dream job will be the one that serves you by taking into account your priorities and giving you the possibility to go after what you are pursuing.

More flexibility, a higher salary, freedom of space – you name it.

Put your well-being first

Don't focus so much on adapting to a role to the extent that you end up compromising your priorities to any lifestyle.

The happiest people are the ones who live up to a vision of success that they have built for themselves and are okay with not fitting into society's standards of what that should mean.

What you had always thought to be your "dream career" might end up not being what you actually want to do in life.

And it's hard to face the feeling of resentment that can come after your mind has sugar-coated the reality of things.

If you listen to yourself closely enough, you will start to develop a sense of intuition that will tell you exactly how you feel about something – sometimes before it even happens.

Numerous times I thought it was probably just a way for my brain to overthink and try to distract me.

But it turned out to be the exact opposite.

You know yourself better than anyone else, so trust your intuition when you're making a decision, and particualrly when you're feeling like you don't belong somewhere anymore.

In my experience, changing jobs has been one of the best ways for me to grow and learn about what I was eager to trade for my career.

Every work opportunity is a chance to learn but also to know yourself better. Take it as it comes.

Be open to growth and most importantly always ask yourself if you like the direction in which you are heading.

If you don't, it's probably time to make a change.

Making a change

Sometimes leaving a job almost feels like abandoning a safe environment, especially when you're in a good place and surrounded by great people.

I know people who have compared it to going through a break-up, after spending maybe five or seven years within the same team and company.

It makes sense. You pick up your habits and find your comfort zone within your routine, and the years keep passing and passing.

But are you really working towards something that excites you?

Or did you just get used to the comfort provided to you within the workplace?

Of course, everyone's situation is different, and so are our priorities, but if you're aiming towards growth you'll need to be a bit selfish when it comes to making career decisions.

When you're starting out as a new hire after completing college, your goal is often to get your first job and gather experience that will be relevant on your CV.

It is often challenging to land that first job after college, and that's why so many graduates end up staying in that role for years, even though the company might not be rewarding their contributions in the right way.

I was fascinated when I learned that changing jobs in Europe brings an average of 22–25% increase on a candidate's salary vs a 3 to 5% increase annually by staying at their current company.

And this is information that people should know independently from their life choices and ambitions.

Whatever career you are aiming for, always be open to explore other options, because even if you're not thinking of leaving, the truth is that every company is subject to external factors that might affect its turnover, market share, and employee headcount.

Or in other words, nobody is ever 100% safe from layoffs.

Companies *do* make staff cuts

Let me share with you a misconception I had about layoffs when I was a student.

I thought companies mainly fired people because they didn't perform up to business metrics or did not meet managerial expectations.

I knew other people were often fired for misbehaving within the workplace, and I was aware that companies had specific codes of conduct to prevent such experiences.

But did anybody warn me about the fact that you could be an excellent employee and go above and beyond for your business unit, do extra projects, take on more responsibilities, yet still be fired?

It almost feels like one of those friendships where you give, and give, and give, and they still end up turning their back on you and not speaking to you anymore.

The feeling of betrayal and resentment feels bitter in the mouth when you see someone close to you experience that, when they poured their heart and soul into that position.

But that doesn't have to be you, if you understand this right now.

A company is a business entity that operates with the aim of making money and serving its costumers – and anything else that might be part of their values.

But primarily, the goal is cashflow.

The biggest companies that are publicly listed on the stock market release their earnings every year, where they disclose their gains and losses compared to the previous year and are obliged to take critical business decisions accordingly.

This could involve suppressing certain departments, reducing budgets, stopping some projects, closing some business units because they are either non-profitable or not currently in the scope of development anymore.

You name it, the message is that companies make decisions based on their own interest.

Now the question is: *why shouldn't you?*

We are often so tied to the concept of company loyalty that we have inherited from the past, that it almost feels wrong to consider other opportunities when we are working somewhere that provides us with stability.

But in life, and within your professional career, nothing is guaranteed and nobody owes you anything.

The sooner you understand this, the less weight you will place upon your own shoulders, and the more free you'll feel in navigating your own path.

The concept of company loyalty

Your employer pays you a salary in exchange for the job you deliver to the company. But if you stopped performing the job, they would stop paying you as well.

It's a mutual contract, where each side has their responsibilities and obligations.

That's how things work, and companies in the 21st century have done a very good job at complementing and breaking up this compensation into *benefits*.

Free snacks, free gym, unlimited holidays, free lunches or discounts.

In today's job market, companies are doing everything in their power to maximise employee retention, or make sure that they're not losing their talent to the competition.

And that brings us to the concept of company loyalty.

There has been a huge shift in our society towards the term "company loyalty", which was a very common term in our parents' and grandparents' lives.

People used to stay at companies for 15+ years, or spend their whole careers in the same field or unit.

That worked for them, and it still works for some people nowadays.

But our generation is more curious to try out new things out, more eager to take risks, and leans towards seeking additional rewards within our professional career.

And that makes us eager to switch careers, change jobs, try out a new profession, or move overseas for a new role.

We have shifted into a world of experience where stability almost seems to be placed second, while people seek growth through change and development.

It is essential that, As a new candidate, it is essential that you understand that while you do your best within your current role, you will need to keep an eye on your own perspectives of evolution.

Do not feel bad for doing this; it's completely natural, and it's a concept that is becoming more and more normalised.

Don't miss out on your own development, keep networking, and be open to new professional beginnings.

You'll thank yourself down the line.

Chapter 10

Navigating Today's Job Market

Entering today's job market as a new graduate is most certainly a crazy experience.

You often have the certifications, the theoretical skills, the grades and accomplishments on paper, only to find out that there are a whole lot of skills required for a position.

And that you're competing with a huge amount of people out there.

Most entry-level positions listed on LinkedIn require a minimum of two years' experience and offer a low starting salary.

Contradiction at its finest, you might say, but companies are really turning into a practice-oriented approach instead of relying on prestigious degrees.

And this is something that you might use in your own favour, so get practical as early as you can.

Internships are an excellent way of doing this, but so is putting yourself out there.

When I was a student, I met some very smart people who had mastered the ability of putting themselves out on the market, before they even had the qualifications to back up their skills.

Find your strengths and transform them into skills

A very common concept within the job market is that you need experience in order to get a job. But you also need to get a job so that you can gather the right experience… to apply for another job.

It turns out this is a neverending circle, unless you find your own ways of creating experience before landing your first full-time position.

Every one of us is born with a specific skillset, numerous passions, and sometimes even gifts, within a certain domain.

You could be passionate about computers and start coding in your free time, or be meticulously good at grammar and help your friends out with their papers, CVs, and cover letters.

You could also be extremely good with design and assembling documents, and enjoy doing it in your free time.

These are all little bits of incredible skills that can be turned into valuable experience, but only if you look at things from a different perspective.

The confident student's perspective.

The one who knows that what they offer is valuable to the market, and that they could get a compensation out of it.

Of course, it might not become your main source of income (or maybe it will), but it will bring you an additional source of revenue besides building up your portfolio of experience for the future.

We are often taught to do things in a specific order – getting that degree so that you can apply for jobs – but we forget that the very beginning of economics was based on people trading goods, which then became services.

You can most certainly be a student and start building your expertise in a specific field; it doesn't have to be one or the other.

Monetise your skills

There are several ways to make money in our times. The internet has opened a wide range of possibilities when it comes to access to knowledge, and to people.

The concept of safety is something that pushes many individuals to live in a state of apprehension and fear of taking risks.

On average, only a minority of people will take the risk of looking foolish, being rejected, or failing at something, while most will settle for less than they are happy with just to avoid such feelings.

As a student, you'll never have a better time for learning and making mistakes than you have now.

When you're still in your early 20s, the world is full of people who have more experience than you and started their careers later than you did.

Most companies I have worked with are often fascinated to see young people taking the lead on business-related topics, and even more when students are the ones leading their own initiative.

A student who displays a great knowledge of his/her skillset and who has found a way to monetise their knowledge is a way better fit for a business position than someone who has graduated with a good degree and zero practical experience.

I often tell this to students I speak with. Sometimes you can't find the right experience, so you will have to make something out of the current circumstances and create it.

If you are passionate about doing certain things, do them out of passion and gather people's testimonials until you have solid social proof that you are *good*.

Once you do, you can start looking for companies that are seeking that service, then charge a lower price than what it would cost them to hire a full-time employee.

There will never be a better time for you to experience building an offer and assessing your service's fit to the market than now.

Build a skill, practise it well, and gather social proof.

You might stumble upon a goldmine. And if not, that's a story to tell on your next interview.

Network like crazy

If the job market was a car, networking would be the accelerator.

Nothing brings a car to full speed more than accelerating through your own path.

So does networking.

Imagine two different people.

Both are excellent students, have a proven track record of successful internships within big companies, and have excellent recommendations from their supervisors.

One of them has been practising the art of networking by attending seminars, business events, and developing a whole bunch of connections on professional platforms such as LinkedIn.

He has shared his accomplishments with industry experts, scheduled coffee chats with sector leaders, and can now leverage a network of experienced professionals for recommendations or job referrals.

The other one has kept his accomplishments to himself, and is now trying to apply for a new role within a company where he has no connections.

Which one would you rather be?

Networking is the most underrated skill of our times. And the internet has made it easily accessible and free, as long as you take the lead and stay consistent in connecting with others.

There will never be a better time to start building your own network than yesterday… oh well, today.

The common mistake people make about developing connections is the belief that they will only have to do so once they *need* to.

But networking works backwards, and you must certainly develop connections with people out of the genuine interest to learn about their role, story, and experience.

And when the time is right, they will indirectly be of assistance and open the right doors for you, as you might do for them.

I always tell students that being a good networker is simply being a genuine and caring human being who wants to learn the most from others and is humble enough to share their own mistakes and learnings.

If you can master the art of not caring about what people might think of you, and approaching everyone with the confidence of a ten-year-old, you're pretty much ahead for the rest of your career.

Invest in building your circle, and your circle will build you and open up doors for you.

LinkedIn is an excellent platform to do so, to meet like-minded people and share your own passions and projects.

And mostly, keep an eye on job postings and land the next role you didn't know you wanted.

Always keep yourself up with the job market

The most common statement that people make when they are struggling with a condition, a problem, or a decision, is that they should have thought about it earlier.

People who have neglected their health and suddenly have to learn how to exercise, often regret not taking up that habit when they were healthier.

People who get out of toxic relationships often regret overlooking the red flags they noticed in the beginning, before they started getting attached.

Human beings have a funny tendency of overlooking or delaying things until their neglect catches them with consequences.

That's how things work in your professional life, too.

One day you're happy starting a new job, and the next thing you know is that your department is being reduced in staff, or that your role is going to be made redundant.

This might sound extreme, but I do not want to sugarcoat the reality of things.

Companies make choices based on their results; managers make decisions based on team performance and business strategy.

You should make decisions based on your judgement, wellbeing, and freedom.

I have friends who tell me I am extremely bold to make such statements, whenever we have a conversation.

The same friends have often been at a company where they are unhappy, underpaid, and felt stuck for the past 6–10 years, and it often makes me wonder if being bold really does save you.

GRADUATE

It's simple math, if everyone puts their best interest at heart.

You should always give your best, but also keep in mind that your role could be easily replaced or suppressed, and that's a *harsh* truth that costs several people years of service.

The most practical advice I give those around me is to keep applying and interviewing for roles even if you are employed, and mostly if you are happy within your role. Because that's when you least expect that something might happen.

Some might call it overthinking; I call it preparing for the worst scenario in the best way.

We most certainly can't anticipate the future, but we can make ourselves ready to embrace whatever life throws at us by being aware.

Applying for a role and going through a couple of interviews might have two different outcomes, and none of them is to be neglected.

In the first scenario, it might serve as a guiding point in learning about what the average market is paying for your skillset, and it can be leveraged to ask for a salary increase or a promotion in your next annual review.

In the second scenario, you might realise that you are actually very interested in this new role, and end up getting to the offer stage.

And again, you can either use that as leverage to ask for a promotion internally, by backing your request with a proven track record of your contributions – or take the new offer.

Either way, you're not losing anything.

Your job is not your identity

When FAANG companies announced massive layoffs, most of the roles affected were individuals who had served the company for decades.

Managers, or the ones with the highest wages, the people that it cost more for the company to keep.

Some of them had been so invested in the company's mission for years that they had overlooked many other important things in their lives, taking for granted that their job was a security, something that shaped their identity.

There is an interesting psychology around how some companies aim to increase employee retention by creating an environment where individuals feel stimulated and almost indebted towards the business itself.

This creates a sense of belonging, where your identity is closely shaped by your work environment, which makes it *very* hard to dissociate the two as time passes.

My biggest advice to someone entering the job market right now is to give their very best and be fully open to absorbing information – but keep a clear separation between your job and who you are as a person.

I have always been annoyed by companies that stimulate an environment where a team is referred to as a *family*, as this creates a very unhealthy dynamic that pushes people to not draw the line between *home* and *work*.

Your job is not your family, although it does support you and your family financially.

Your colleagues are not your family; they are people with whom you bond through work relationships, in an established environment.

A temporary professional environment.

Don't let pizza nights convince you that's not the case.

Build your reputation internally

When you are starting a new job, every interaction you will have within your work environment is something to nurture and take very seriously.

As first impressions do last, so does ongoing motivation and curiosity to learn from those around you.

People are used to thinking that networking only happens outside of their company, sector, or business sphere. But the first place for networking is indeed your workplace.

Connect with people from other departments, and use your first months within the company to build your internal network.

The ability to socialise with people, learning from them and making them remember who you are, will help you progress faster than you can imagine in your career.

Offer your help, ask for feedback and guidance, and take the lead on new initiatives.

Being able to connect with others will not only help you build your own place within the company, but you will gain additional trust and responsibility if you constantly show up as someone who gives their best and has everyone's best interest at heart.

Not only that, but when you are aiming for an internal transfer or a potential promotion, you will be surprised about how much being known internally can play out in your favour, simply because you will already have people rooting for you.

Build your own social brand

People connect with people, interact with people, and support people that they trust and admire.

The purpose of a brand is simply that.

Social media has made it extremely simple for people to put themselves out there and specialise in a specific niche, follow that passion that they might have had for the longest time, and inspire others to do the same.

When you start building your brand, you become a go-to person in a specific field or industry, and people will start relating to you and aim to hear your experience, to learn from you.

Before you realise it, you are slowly building what will become your social brand.

Building a social brand within the professional world is an incredibly powerful asset that will open a multitude of doors for you, and help you gain authority within your industry.

A social brand is simply what I define as a virtual handshake.

People might not know you personally, but they directly associate your knowledge and skills with something that you specifically post or talk about.

One of my biggest investments within my professional career was building and developing a brand for myself on LinkedIn, through consistent posting and networking.

I had initially been a passive user of LinkedIn, only connecting from time to time and consuming some content.

OnceIi started treating my LinkedIn profile as my brand page, everything changed.

I started sharing content about specific topics that resonated with my experience, and I slowly transitioned from 200 to 20,000 followers in a couple of months.

Further down the line, I had the chance to meet incredible people, be invited to the LinkedIn HQ, attend podcasts, speak at some of the biggest universities in Europe, attend international events as a speaker, and more.

That's when I started realising how much of an impact it can have to build an audience that supports your journey, trusts your opinion, and sees you as an inspiration in their own career path.

The incredible advantage that the internet gives us nowadays is that you don't need to be an expert at anything in order to get started. You just need to be motivated enough to make an impact.

And once you get started, the rest will slowly unfold.

You are the biggest project you will ever work on

There is a quote I heard in a podcast that changed my whole perception about work, career, and personal achievements.

It's from Jim Rohn – one of my favorite motivational speakers – stating that you need to *work harder on yourself than you work on your job.*

I remember walking with an episode of his podcast playing in my ears, when this sentence got me stopping the audio to think about what he'd said for a couple minutes.

And it made so much sense for me that I couldn't look at things the same anymore.

We are so conditioned to think that we need to be successful in the things we have to do, that we often forget how essential it is to work on becoming *our* best version.

So many external factors will keep demanding effort and energy from you: projects to deliver, deadlines to meet, your next promotion, and everything that comes in between.

And we make it our mission to over-achieve and over-deliver in order to get to the next steps.

But how often do we sit down with ourselves and think of all the ways we could improve *our own* day-to-day lives if we set work aside?

Your values, character, habits, and principles are the biggest and most rewarding things you will ever build – simply because they set the base for everything else you will think of, aim for, and do in your life.

As simple as it sounds, yet so underrated.

The importance of putting yourself first and investing time into growing as a person is something that should be at the core of your focus.

There is no finish line

How often do we find ourselves starting something with extreme excitement about finishing it or getting to the reward phase?

Idealising rewards and not efforts.

Pleasure vs what our brains perceive as pain.

If you ask someone who is preparing to run their first marathon, they will very likely tell you about how excited and impatient they are to cross the finish line.

The feeling of satisfaction, knowing that their work has paid off.

Yet if you ask them after the run happened, they will unconsciously end up telling you more about the journey that got them there, without even realising that the finish line wasn't the whole point.

The same thing happens with our lives.

Human beings tend to crave the end result and picture themselves in those ideal circumstances before the effort and sacrifices even happen.

That's the way we are; our minds idealise situations and things.

It almost feels like an adrenaline rush when we think of ourselves in a specific position, owning a particular item, or finishing a specific project.

The impatient side of us tends to take control, sometimes almost stealing away the magic of the journey itself.

When you are getting started as a young professional, things might often feel the same.

The ambition to succeed, make money, travel the world, get promoted — all of these factors and many more will constantly push you to be impatient for the next *big* thing.

But let me be honest with you, the next big thing is only big before you get there. Then it becomes another piece of the puzzle.

The truth is: *there is no finish line.*

If you seek satisfaction in belongings or professional rewards, you will rarely feel content.

Learn to enjoy the process, embrace the journey, and be grateful for everything that comes with it.

Fall in love with the idea that every experience is shaping you into the person you are meant to become, teaching you new skills, and making you wiser and smarter.

From every experience, learn about what you want – and mostly what you do not want – and once you are ready, trust yourself that it's time to move to the next level.

True success relies in *self-contentment*.

Conclusion

Dear reader,

If you have made it to the end of this book, I would like to thank you for your consistency.

When I started writing *Graduate*, I only had one goal in mind: for it to serve the person who would read it.

I hope this book will be something you come back to when you're facing uncertainty.

I would like you to treat it as a manual, re-read parts of it, make annotations, and use my experience to hopefully make yours easier and smoother.

Remember that every step you'll take in your professional journey will open up a new, exciting chapter.

There is no final destination; take every opportunity as it comes.

And mostly, don't forget to have fun along the way.

Thank you note

To my parents, Bahija and Lahcen, this book is for you.

To my family. Thank you for always supporting me, believing in me and encouraging me to be my best self every day.

I am the most blessed person to be surrounded by your love and affection.

To my best friend Melissa, I am so grateful to have you.

To my dear friends Imane and Amina, thank you for your excitement and feedback during *Graduate*'s publishing process.

Thank you to the publishing team at Grosvenor House Publishing for making the process smooth and bringing *Graduate* to life.

Contact the Author

Dear reader, I would love to hear from you.

Let's connect on my LinkedIn @Soukayna Ikhiche.

Until the next lecture,

Soukayna